Little Teachers

BETSY HENNY

Little Teachers

Copyright ©2023 Betsy Henny

ISBN   979-8-9886105-0-2   Softcover
ISBN   979-8-9886105-1-9   Hardcover
ISBN   979-8-9886105-2-6   eBook

Cover photo by Paul Henny

Author photo by Beth Preston Photography

Book design by Nan Barnes, StoriesToTellBooks.com

Little Teachers

Contents

This book is dedicated to

My Mother . . .

Who gave me wings,
and showed me the sky

Joshua and Brittany . . .

Who lifted me up.

Paul . . .
Who is the wind beneath my wings.

And all my Little Teachers
who through the years
sparkled like stars in the heavens,
and forever twinkle in my heart.

INTRODUCTION

I do not recall making a calculated decision to go into the teaching profession. I guess, like everyone else, there were many changes of plans. Each time that I thought with certainty, "I know what I want to be when I grow up," I would change my mind. I had so many interests. There was cooking, gardening, and music. I also enjoyed painting, sewing, crafts, and writing. In school, the subjects of psychology, history, science, and literature were always my favorites. It was just so difficult to pinpoint one particular area of interest. Then I realized that, woven throughout all I enjoyed doing, was one common thread—my love for children.

I grew up in rural Southern Virginia. My early years were filled with playing in the creek, haylofts, running with calves, and making mud pies in the sandbox. I was so fortunate to have my grandparents right next door. I followed my grandfather around as he tended to the cows. I learned how to bale hay and raise a garden. Then, in the house with Grandmother, I learned to sew on an old foot-pedal Singer sewing machine. Pushing a stool up to the counter, I learned to pat out biscuits before I ever started school. I learned how to set a proper table and starch a linen tablecloth.

There was always music. Granddaddy played the fiddle and the banjo, so I was raised with foot-stompin' bluegrass pulsing through my veins. I began playing a piano before my hands could stretch to reach five keys of an octave.

There wasn't any preschool or kindergarten except for those who wished to seek out private institutions, so I didn't start school until I was almost seven years old. In one year's time, I learned my letters, sounds, adding, subtracting, and how to read fluently in a setting with thirty other children. I loved school and was unaware at the time that my beloved first-grade teacher was having a great impact on me. She controlled the entire class with ease while never raising her voice above a calm speaking tone. We loved and respected her. Misbehaving was not an option.

As my elementary years gave way to high school, I took on many part-time jobs. The first and foremost in my mind was the summer my mother put me to work in a factory. It was hot and boring. I remember walking around a table, correlating sections for a catalog all day, every day. Boredom was my mother's intention. She wanted me to desire with all my heart to go to college. I would have to take out loans to pay for it, but after that summer, I gladly added college to my plans for the future.

Throughout my college experience, I worked at daycares, summer-camp programs, and private babysitting. I realized that I had a way with children. I found them fascinating, and for reasons unknown to me, they found me captivating.

It was in my junior year in college that I chose teaching. It was like an epiphany. What a perfect opportunity to utilize all my interests, talents, and natural abilities into my profession.

As fate should have it, my very first job assignment was in the school I had attended as an intermediate-grade student, which at that time had housed sixth and seventh grades. Now I was the new kindergarten teacher, and I was ecstatic!

I started right off bringing everything into the classroom that I had enjoyed as a child. I designed lessons centered around music, cooking, and the great outdoors. I made my own bulletin boards to make the classroom warm and inviting. We had art and music every day, and most importantly, we had love in that little room. I listened to what the children told me about their lives, and together, we made sense of the great big world. They learned that my classroom was a place where they were respected and treasured as the dear little people they were. They felt safe and loved.

As I saw the years speeding by, I began to keep a journal. I knew without a doubt that I was on sacred ground with these children and that someday, I needed to share it with the world. I felt that I had the greatest profession there was: spending my days with amazing little people.

Each year that went by, I met a few more children who would get entries in my journal. I never felt the time was right to close the door and write my book.

I suppose I'd always wondered just what would be the catalyst. Just what would finally puff wind in my sails and set me off on this book-writing venture of mine. I had kept notes and journals for thirty-one years. It was always "someday." Someday, I was going to tell everyone what actually went on in that classroom. Finally, parents everywhere would get to read with laughs and tears what took place behind those doors. I had always prayed that God would just tap me on the shoulder and tell me the time had come.

When it finally happened, it was actually more dramatic than that. God provided the blank notebook, with a portion of the introduction already written. From the pen of my sixteen-year-old son, a poem was etched on the first page. I came across it while cleaning the closet. My breath caught in my throat because then I knew—the time was *now*.

From My Childhood, by Josh Rodgers

Gripping the seat of our old car, I would plead and beg my mother to let me miss kindergarten that day. I was too scared to leave her. I didn't know what would happen or what to expect, even though every day was the same. But she would always have a way of telling me everything was going to be all right.

Next thing you know, I would be walking into my little school, feeling invincible. . . .

So there I had it. Told to me by my own son. My job as a teacher was to instill that feeling of security and power into each of my students. That inner peace was what enabled them to learn. But more importantly, it enabled them to teach. For what I taught children is not what this book is about. It is about what I learned from them. True learning, I believe, is not only about what you take in but what you internalize and are able to share with others, and I want the whole world to know what I learned from my "Little Teachers."

My dream for this book is to convey to aspiring teachers, to new parents, and to anyone who will just take a moment to let the idea sink in, that children have a lot to teach us.

If parents are picking up this book to see if I wrote about their child, please realize that I did. However, with the exception of a few, their names have been changed so you will not know anyone's identity for certain. This was on purpose. Every child I have ever taught made an impact on me in some way. They are all in my heart.

Hopefully, as you read, you will laugh, and you will cry, just as I did throughout the years.

Be sure to read my section intitled, After Class, where you will get to see what has become of a few of my Little Teachers. For just as they were amazing little people, they have become just as amazing as adults.

PREFACE

You are about to enter my classroom. I'd love for you to sit a spell with each student and reflect on the remarkable little person each one was.

It was an absolute joy to teach during the era in which I taught. For most of my career, I was allowed to go above and beyond the curriculum and engage my students in cooking, social skills and manners, music, art, sewing, and individualizing instruction to meet the many learning styles.

These children loved to talk, and I loved to listen. I laughed and cried a lot, and together, we learned. I hope you can feel the love that was in that little classroom. And I also hope you will take away some lessons from my wonderful Little Teachers.

Leah

I always think of her as my very first student. Even though I had twenty-four that year, she was the first one I met. Her mother actually called me on the phone and arranged to take me out to lunch one day during the week before the school year started. She wanted to get to know the person who would be entrusted with her baby. I'm serious. This really happened.

Looking back, I remember thinking that I had chosen the best profession in the world. Getting to spend my days with incredible children and having their parents take me out to lunch was going to be awesome. It turns out that I was 50 percent correct, for I never got treated to lunch again, but spending my days with children for thirty-one years definitely made up for it.

After the lunch date, when this wonderful mom confessed her fears of sending her baby out into the world, and I assured her of my fierce maternal instincts to protect her as my own, I met Leah. She was a tiny clone of her mother—waist-length, milk-chocolate hair, deep puppy-brown eyes, a petite build, and a shy smile. Unlike her mom though, she had a sprinkling of freckles across her nose, which crinkled when she laughed. It was meeting

Leah that made it all very real to me. It was a sobering realization, too. I was to have not only Leah, but twenty-three others just like her in my care for several hours a day. I was responsible for getting them prepared for the next rung in their academic ladder. I had to teach them rules, and skills, and manners. For many, I would be the first person other than their families to care for them. I would have to help them make a comfortable transition.

Then, while looking at those trusting brown eyes, came the gravest realization of all. Although hopefully it would never happen, I could be the determining factor in saving these children in a life-or-death situation.

So began my teaching career that spanned thirty-one years.

Leah settled into her new schedule virtually problem free. She found that if she was a little homesick, I'd rock it away in my rocking chair. If her hair got in the way, I would braid it up in a fancy "do." If she had trouble opening something at lunch, I was right there to help. Learning the alphabet and counting was fun because she had so many friends learning along with her. And while all this was going on, I was also learning. I was developing a teaching style that would eventually be my trademark. Reaching back into my own childhood experiences in the kitchen with my mother and grandmother, I brought cooking into the classroom. I watched and discovered that children learn more quickly when you utilize materials from their familiar environment. We were outdoors every possible day, walking, exploring, getting dirty, and allowing our five senses to work together to learn about this big wonderful world.

During a lot of that year, I was learning as much as the children. I well remember the very first day of school, when it was time to go to breakfast. I dutifully told the class to get in line. A child, very puzzled, asked me, "Where is a lion?"

I laughed and told them they had misunderstood me. I repeated a little more clearly, "Please get into a line." The puzzled looks on their faces spelled out the reality for me. They did not know what that meant. Getting into a line was something I had to teach them to do.

Little Leah still stands out among the others that year because of a valuable lesson she taught me. I was her mommy when her mommy wasn't there. That alone was a huge responsibility, not only to Leah, but also to all the other children who basically felt the same way.

Then came the morning when Leah did not come to school. It was a beautiful Monday following an equally beautiful weekend. I had planned a lesson that would get us outdoors into the sunshine.

A call came into the office for me from Leah's mother. "Good morning, Janet," I greeted her and immediately inquired about Leah.

She awkwardly began her story as to why Leah was not in school. It seems that she and her family had spent a day at a nearby park where there is a lovely lake and beach. I knew it well. It was one of my favorite spots to go to with friends. In fact, I had also been there over the weekend.

"Yes," Janet replied. "We saw you there. And that's the problem. Leah saw you in your bathing suit, and for whatever reason, it has upset her greatly. Maybe it was just too much skin for her," she joked. "I tried talking to her but she has just taken to her bed. I think she thought you lived at school and that is all you do."

"Oh gracious." We both had to share a hearty laugh, but then we had to address the problem. I asked to speak to Leah on the phone. Leah answered very weakly on the other end. I told her I missed her, and I was hoping she would be back tomorrow. Then I talked about the park where we had been and I expressed how much I would like to swim there with her sometime. That seemed to do the trick and she perked up immediately. It was a real puzzle. It was if she had to bridge a gap between my life at school with her and this unfamiliar life I appeared to have—a life without her. A life with grown friends away from school and in different clothes.

I went one step further. After getting off the phone with her, I planned my end-of-the-year field trip. I took my whole class to that park, and we also covered the dam and reservoir close by. It was a lovely day of picnicking, swimming, and learning that teachers are people too.

What a valuable lesson learned. While teachers are also "regular people," we have a responsibility to our students and their families to always keep our behavior and appearance above reproach. Little eyes tend to put us on a pedestal, and that isn't such a bad thing—as long as we make sure we don't fall off.

Lamar

I was still classified as a new teacher. It was just my third year, so I was tweaking my style, learning the ropes, and adding to my bag of tricks. And I was about to meet the little boy who was going to teach me a lesson that I would carry to the end of my career.

His name was Lamar. Big, brown eyes, black, curly hair, deep dimples, and as mischievous as the day is long. I could tell quite early on that he had not had a lot of discipline. It wasn't that he came from an uncaring family. His parents were interested in Lamar and concerned that he do well. I think it was just that there were so many children in that household that he more or less slipped through the cracks.

He was smart, a quick thinker, and sneaky. Thankfully, he wasn't aggressive with the other children, but he was disruptive and antagonistic. He would do everything he could just short of hitting his classmates. For that restraint, I was thankful, yet my days seemed to be increasingly occupied with settling squabbles with Lamar in the middle.

But between his unscrupulous behaviors, Lamar was a charmer. He knew how to say, "Good Morning," with a hint of pure maple syrup. He would rush to a door with a "Let me help you with that." A day never passed that I didn't hear a compliment from him about my hair, my clothes, or even my lessons. He would say they were "very interesting."

The principal of our little school was pushing the age of retirement. The staff adored him and I, particularly, viewed him as a father figure. He had actually known my daddy, so I think he was personally looking out for me as I began my teaching career. He overlooked a lot. Like the time I took my class on a two-mile nature walk down the path from the school. We visited a little market where I bought juices for the kids and then walked back.

He was waiting for me outside his office, his hands on his hips. "Where have you been?" he asked, scratching his chin. After I cheerfully described our adventure, he rubbed the top of his balding head. "You just went on a field trip. From now on, you have to get approval and permission slips." I remember he smiled and never brought it up again.

On another occasion, he called me out in the hall when he heard me praying with my class before lunch. I was always careful to never force anyone to pray. I simply told the class that I was going to ask the blessing, and if anyone wanted to join me, they could.

"Now, Miss Plaster, I'm totally on your side with you praying with the kids and teaching them they can pray and all that. But if someone ever complains to the superintendent or the school board, you must realize that I can't help you out." He breathed a heavy sigh and waited for my response.

"Well, sir," I said, weighing my words carefully. "I would rather get called on the carpet down here for doing it than to get called on the carpet up there"—as I pointed to heaven—"for not doing it."

I remember he smiled and never mentioned that again, either.

So, with him having previously offered me all that guidance, naturally, I turned to him for help with Lamar.

The day had been especially stressful. Lamar had continually kept something going. He had pulled a chair out and caused a classmate to fall. He had taken a toy truck away from a child during center time. He had scribbled on another child's paper. Time out hadn't worked. Phone calls to his parents had been ineffective. Exasperated, I led Lamar to Mr. Jones to ask direction. I was new at this and wanted to do things right.

Mr. Jones stood up from his office chair, walked around, and sat on the edge of his desk, facing Lamar. I could tell he was having a difficult time keeping a straight face as he looked at this "Little Rascal" look-alike. Lamar was standing solemnly, eyes wide, listening to the accusations facing him.

Mr. Jones tried to be stern. "Lamar," he said. "Miss Plaster tells me you haven't been behaving in the classroom. Can you tell me why you didn't do what Miss Plaster asked you to do?"

Lamar's eyes met Mr. Jones's. Then they shifted to mine. He quickly averted his gaze back to his judge. He knew his fate rested in the principal's hands, so this had to be good. "Because," Lamar said, "she didn't say please."

Well, there you have it. Guilty as charged. I admit . . . I did not say please.

Lamar, my "Little Rascal," you taught me the very basic foundation of all proper instruction: remember to always say please and thank you. After all, if you want respect, you have to also give it.

Anthony

This story will be different from all the others in this book. You won't discover the lesson I learned from Anthony until you read his After Class chapter.

Anthony wasn't technically a student of mine. He was in the emotionally disturbed class housed in a classroom at the opposite end of the hall. He tended to have somewhat violent outbursts from time to time. Heaven only knows what that child's home-life was like. He was tall for his seven years, with dark-brown hair that often obscured the most troubled eyes I have ever seen on a child. I found that I couldn't look into them very long. He seemed to lack all emotion and it reflected in his stare.

It was somewhat customary for Anthony's teacher to send him to my room when he needed some decompression time. I never knew what he had done. I just received him at my door, and sometimes, he had some work to do and I set him up in a quiet corner of the room to do it.

On this particular day, Anthony arrived at the beginning of rest time. I could tell by his expression that he was not overjoyed at being brought down. I fixed him a mat on the floor with the rest of my class and gave him a blanket. As was my custom, I closed the blinds, put on a Johnny Mathis record, and went to my desk to do paperwork amidst all the snoring.

What needs to be added here is that I was seven months pregnant with my little girl. I was "great with child," and by rest time each day, I was ready to sit a spell.

My sitting didn't last long on this day. I smelled smoke. I turned and raised the blind slightly to see if the janitor was burning any debris outside. The odor definitely wasn't the usual coal smell from our furnace. I didn't see any smoke, so I quickly turned my attention to the darkened room. Keeping the blind raised slightly to allow some light to filter in, I began my walk around the room. All the children were sleeping peacefully, their little cheeks looking so rosy against their blue mats. But then I came to Anthony's mat, and not only did I not see him, but the smell of smoke was strong. The towel I had given him was pulled completely up over his head, covering his entire body.

I reached down and pulled the towel off him. Anthony was lying on his back, a cigarette lighter in one hand and a charred piece of paper in the other. Our eyes met. His glare was cold and I didn't have a second to react. He pulled both legs up to his chin and, with one violent thrust, sent his feet into my pregnant belly. I gasped, and holding my stomach with one hand and grabbing Anthony with the other, I got him on his feet.

There was a blur of activity after that. Anthony was whisked away to the office and an aide was called to my class. I had to go to the emergency room and receive medication to stop labor because the trauma had started contractions. The medical intervention was successful, and I went on to carry my daughter full term.

I never had any more contact with Anthony that year. The elementary school closed months later and teachers and students were sent to the two other elementary schools in the area. My next encounter with Anthony would not happen for four more years.

Kasey H.

I have always believed that anything worthwhile is worth working hard for. I also believe "that which doesn't kill us makes us stronger." Those beliefs were proven true the year I had Kasey. The end of that year definitely found me a much stronger woman.

When I met Kasey, I already knew her mother, father, and older sister. I knew Kasey's mom to be a strong Christian woman, very active in her church, and the household was run under strict Bible discipline. So when Rose showed up on registration day to put Kasey in my classroom, I felt lucky. Here was a child I was certain would be well behaved.

She was so cute. Wispy brown curls of hair surrounded a freckled face. Blue, translucent eyes, so light they just offered a trace of color. Whenever she smiled, she shyly looked down, as if it embarrassed her. Yes, I thought, Kasey would be delightful.

I'm not sure what the first incident was. There were so many that they ran together like Seattle fog. It could have been when she bit a classmate in center time, or when she cut her hair, or she cut Dylan's hair or the doll's hair. Or it could very well be when she told Stephanie she was going to punch her in the stomach, then did so. And it could have been when she hid in the coatroom under a towel, and I searched and called everywhere, causing panic throughout the school until she came out laughing. It doesn't really matter which was the first incident, because it certainly wasn't the last. But delightful wasn't the word I used to describe Kasey anymore, at least not all the time.

Regardless, I loved her. In between her moments on the dark side, she was precious. She would run up to me, wrap her arms around me, and say, "I just love you so much." She would rush to help me carry out supplies. She would clean the sink after painting. She would stack all the mats after rest time. Somehow, I had to encourage more of that side of Kasey to shine.

Her mother and father were horrified at the calls, notes, and conferences. Now, notice that I didn't say "surprised." This was the Kasey they knew. They were just horrified that she was doing these things at school. Kasey was just an extremely strong-willed child. We all just needed to find a form of discipline that worked for her. Nothing so far, at home or at school, did.

Then came the day there was no reprieve. From the moment Kasey bounded off the school bus, there was much chaos and gnashing of teeth. Children were crying because Kasey had slapped, pushed, or hit them. There were crayon markings all over the bathroom wall, duti-fully signed with Kasey's name. The principal handed me a bus referral to go home to Kasey's parents because she had thrown a child's lunchbox out the window that morning.

Oh my goodness! I had to do something different. What I had been doing to this point was not working. Suddenly, a new idea popped into my head. Kasey had been brought up in the church and lived in a home where the family read the Bible together daily. This was so similar to my own upbringing, and I knew what had kept me in line as a child. "Kasey," I called. "Would you please come here?"

She came straight to me, shoulders down, face sullen, a look I was seeing more often now.

"Kasey, I want to talk to you," I began. "You've been getting into trouble a whole lot and having to be punished so much of the time that you're missing out on so many fun activities. Kasey, I know you love Jesus and want to make Him happy. Jesus doesn't want you to behave like this at school. Don't you want to start doing what Jesus wants you to do?"

I stopped. It was now Kasey's turn to respond. I felt confident that this was the necessary route and that this would work. I almost felt the exhilaration of success! I searched Kasey's eyes, fully expecting to see the rush of remorse and feel those little arms fling around my neck as she begged forgiveness from me *and* Jesus.

Without moving her gaze away from my eyes, she spoke. "I want to go to Hell and see the Devil."

I'm not really sure what emotion I felt at that moment, but I think the closest label I could put on it was fear. "I see," I managed to say and slowly stood. I moved backward, away from her, almost as one who backs away from a coiled snake. I needed to think about what to do next, and I couldn't do it here, beside Kasey, when she wanted to visit the Devil.

Sometimes, the best plan of action is to do nothing. Waiting is a strategy that works well, and I have used it in dealing with many stressful decisions in my life. Sometimes, the best answer comes if you wait for it. And so I did . . . and so it came. Not that day, or even the day after. Kasey continued her rampages, intermingled with her endearing sweetness and devotion. And then the waiting paid off. From deep back in the crevices of my memory, I recalled something I had heard my daddy say while talking to my mother about a situation they were facing. He had said, "Hilda, you know the best way to egg something on is to oppose the damn thing."

So, there I had it. Maybe Kasey wouldn't want to go to Hell so badly if we told her she could go. And what if we just encouraged her to continue with her itinerary if she wanted to spend more time with her buddy, the Devil.

The next time Kasey chose the low road, which happened very quickly, we had our talk. She had taken black paint and destroyed Peyton's artwork. So, with Peyton sobbing as our backdrop, I pulled Kasey aside. "Kasey, I'm not sending you to time out today."

She looked up at me, and a slight smile seemed to be forming across her little lips. "You're not?" she asked, not believing her good fortune.

"No, absolutely not," I said. "You told me that you wanted to go to Hell and see the Devil, and this is the way you do it. You start off as a little child doing bad things, and when you grow up, you do even worse things until you find that you're in trouble all the time. And that's just what the Devil loves! But, you do know that you don't just visit the Devil. You will have to live with him forever and ever if you choose his ways. And the only people who will be with you are all the other people in the world who wanted to see the Devil. Your mama and daddy won't be there, and I won't be there. We don't like the Devil. So, I've decided that I'm just going to let you do all the mean things you want to do, so it will be much easier for you to see the Devil because that's what you want."

I watched for Kasey's reaction. There was none. She looked like she was frozen in time. Then it was her turn to back away from *me* like I was a coiled snake. Without changing her expression, and without uttering a word, she slowly walked to our little library and plopped down into the beanbag. Poor little thing. She had a lot of thinking to do.

And once again, it was time to wait. Slowly, like spring arriving after a long, cold winter, I saw a change in Kasey. I actually witnessed her stopping herself in the midst of an evil deed or two. I found myself not being exhausted anymore. I started seeing more of the Kasey I adored, and by year's end, little Kasey walked happily on the high road more than the low.

Oh, my little Kasey. She was certainly worth the extra effort, and she once again taught me that waiting with patience is sometimes the single most effective thing we as teachers can do.

Josie

My family tree has twin apples hanging from its branches. So, as a teacher it was never intimidating when two, little, identical faces came walking into my classroom. I could always tell them apart in seconds. The year I had Josie and June was especially uncomplicated. The girls were supposedly identical twins but were not only markedly different in appearance, their personalities and temperaments were a sharp contrast as well.

Both had beautiful, thick, waist-length, golden-brown hair. June liked to have hers pulled back in clips or, sometimes, even a bow. Josie was a free spirit with a heavy sprinkling of tomboy. Her hair was always down, falling at will about her shoulders and down her back. June leaned toward florals and feminine choices when selecting her clothes. Josie preferred jeans and T-shirts. Rarely did they ever dress the same. Both girls, however, were extremely artistic. Horses literally looked as if they could trot off their drawing paper. Trees and flowers surrounded unicorns and castles. I always made sure they had access to any art supplies they needed to create their masterpieces. They both expressed themselves through their art. Being on the shy side, it was difficult to get either to talk more than answering questions. They stuck together most of the time, and although they appeared to be content, they rarely smiled. I always thought they just looked bored, yet their mother reported they loved school and were always eager to come.

I vividly remember the day Josie came to me during naptime. It was a Friday, the week before our kindergarten commencement exercises. She never, ever complained about anything, but the look on her face as she approached me signaled that was about to change. With her hand on her stomach, her words made me feel uneasy. "Mrs. Rodgers, my tummy feels hot."

I slid my hand under hers and rubbed her skin in a circular motion. She didn't feel feverish. "Does your tummy hurt, Josie?" I asked, trying to understand her terminology for "hot."

"No, it just feels hot inside," she repeated.

Our naptime was just before dismissal, so calling her parents to come get her was pointless. She would be home before anyone could get to the school. So I rocked her until snack time and then sent her home on the bus with June. But something just didn't feel right. I thought about the way she said "hot," and for an unexplained reason, I was extremely anxious.

I called her mother, who was waiting for the girls at home. I explained what had happened and alerted her to the possibility that Josie was coming down with something. She thanked me for the heads up and said she would alter their usual Friday night pizza menu. Possibly "bland" should be their precautionary choice.

My weekend was busy as I prepared for the last full week of school. I filled out the children's diplomas and awards and planned the refreshments for our closing ceremony. It was certainly a time for reflection, and I was so proud of all my students. As always, I felt a twinge of sadness at the thought of saying goodbye to my babies.

At school on Monday morning, I wasn't surprised that Josie and June were absent. I surmised that it was a stomach bug and guessed that by now the entire family had taken ill.

When Tuesday came and still no twins, my concern heightened, and I called and left a message. The return call for me came into the office on Wednesday morning, and nothing could have prepared me for what I was about to hear. It was Josie and June's daddy on the phone. "Mrs. Rodgers," he began with a tone that prompted me to take a seat. "We have some really bad news." Josie had continued with her complaints through the weekend of her stomach being "hot." By Sunday, she was in pain and they had made a trip to the ER. The nightmare began with the results of a sonogram. Josie had a growing mass in her ovary and further testing had concluded the worst. It was cancerous.

I remember struggling to comprehend it all. Mr. Hancock explained that the mass was composed of teeth, hair, and bone fragments of a third child. June and Josie were to have been triplets, but the third baby never completely formed. For five years the bones and tissues had been dormant in little Josie's body. But the evil beast had awakened and was growing and spreading at an alarming speed. Surgery would be performed right away. But first, Josie wanted to graduate from kindergarten with June. He said he and his wife would be bringing them for the ceremony then leaving for the hospital right away.

I thanked him for the call, offered my prayers for Josie and their whole family, hung up the phone, and wept.

Friday came and I had prepared myself for the twins' arrival. I had made a get-well bag for Josie and a comfort bag for June with puzzles, stuffed animals, coloring books, and crayons. I forbade myself to show any tears around Josie and prayed for the help I would need to follow through.

As I led my class into the gym for the ceremony, the Hancocks had not yet arrived. Had Josie taken a turn for the worse? I seated the children, leaving two empty chairs just in case.

At that moment I saw the family appear in the doorway. The girls came running to me, and I embraced them in a hug. As Josie wrapped her arms around my neck, her little tummy pressed into mine. I felt a chill run through my body like an electrical jolt. Where only a week before she had complained of feeling hot, there was now a fist-sized growth that was like a rock. It had jagged edges protruding angrily under Josie's soft skin. It felt evil, and vile, and alien. I silently cursed it under my breath for invading this innocent child.

I glanced at her parents standing together at the back of the gym, tears streaming down their faces. Their daughter's future at this point, on this day, was uncertain. She would graduate with her sister from kindergarten. But what about middle school, high school, and college?

I walked to the podium and began calling names. As June and Josie received their diplomas, they hugged me and immediately joined their parents at the door. Mr. and Mrs. Hancock offered a somber wave, and then they disappeared out the door. I was left to finish the ceremony, forced to keep a smile on my face for all the families oblivious to the horror the Hancocks were experiencing.

The following week was a blur. Josie was in surgery for several hours and the doctors were optimistic that all of the mass had been removed. Chemotherapy began immediately and once again Josie's body was invaded and wracked with nausea.

I had completed the school year and our following workweek, so I made plans to make the three-hour trip to visit Josie. With a teddy bear and a drawing tablet in hand, I entered the sprawling hospital. I exited the elevator on the children's floor and began my search for Josie's room. As I walked the long hallway, I passed sunny windows and colorful murals. There was a big, open playroom with toys and beanbag chairs and tricycles. All of the happy images were in sharp contrast to the pale, bald children in hospital gowns seated in wheelchairs and parents' laps. Was I prepared to see Josie?

Quite unexpectedly, I found myself directly in front of the room that matched the sweaty slip of paper in my hand. I took a deep breath, put a smile on my face, and pushed open the door.

I was happily greeted by Mr. and Mrs. Hancock, who rose from their chairs and embraced me with hugs and grateful handshakes. But where was Josie? For lying in the middle of the stark white sheets was a tiny form unfamiliar to me. Eyes closed in sleep, there were no golden-brown strands of hair falling about her shoulders. The skin was shiny in appearance, and an angry-looking IV was taped to her wisp of an arm. I quickly turned my eyes back to Mr. and Mrs. Hancock, hoping the cheery smiles that greeted me were still there. They were not. They had been replaced with a mysterious stare that I never want to experience again. The stare of broken-hearted parents as they searched the eyes of everyone who looked at their daughter to see if they held the same fear theirs did.

They whispered that she had just been medicated and would probably sleep for a while longer. I left my gifts and exited to grab lunch, saying I would return in an hour or so.

Turns out, there wasn't anything in the cafeteria I thought I could swallow except a cup of coffee. How could I eat when little Josie looked like that?

Watching the clock and reflecting on my year with Josie, I realized just what it is that I love so dearly about teaching. I become fiercely attached to these children. A bond develops and they are like family. I closed my eyes there in that bustling cafeteria amid the sick and the well and prayed for my family member to be healed.

After about an hour and a half, I returned to her hospital room. Pushing the door slightly open, I saw Josie propped up on pillows with the big drawing tablet open in front of her. She looked up at me and an ever-so-shy smile spread across her face.

"Oh, Josie," I said cheerfully. "May I see what you're drawing?" I walked to her bedside and peeked over. There, as if it could whinny, was a beautiful horse, mane blowing in a fantasy breeze.

With her eyes open, I could see the Josie I knew.

I stayed for a while longer, and I didn't have to fake my cheerfulness. Seeing her up and smiling gave me assurance that all would be well. I left the hospital with a deep sense of relief and gratitude, thankful for the skilled doctors, gratitude for God's grace and mercy, and appreciation for seeing a miracle here on earth.

The cancer had been eradicated from Josie's body and she recovered. After a year of homebound instruction for both girls, a precaution against infections, Josie was deemed cancer free. She returned to school the following year, sporting a short bob of hair and loving her baseball caps.

The whole experience is one I will draw on for the rest of my life. John Bradford's phrase, "There but for the grace of God go I," was etched on my soul. As the mother of two children, one of them Josie's age, I felt the helplessness Josie's parents had felt. We must always love and cherish our children and family each day enough to last a lifetime. We never know how long that lifetime will be.

Emanuel

I was just beginning my eleventh year of teaching. It was getting much easier. By now, bulletin boards had been designed and created for every season and unit. I had stored all types of handmade manipulatives. Lesson plans had been written and filed for easy access. I was successfully juggling teaching with raising two kindergarten-aged children of my own. I had met and handled every level of challenge in my classroom up to this point. So, on the morning that our ESL teacher, Miss Wine, came into my classroom with a new student, I braced myself to tackle uncharted territory.

I spoke no Spanish. In high school I had taken three years of French but had forgotten most of that. Miss Wine took me aside and told that my new student was coming from Atlanta, spoke no English, and was living with his aunt. His mother and father were still in Georgia. She assured me that after she made her rounds to the other rooms, she would return to help me get Emanuel settled. Her case load was so large that she couldn't promise more assistance than that.

I took Emanuel to an empty desk and placed a color

sheet in front of him. All of my students had morning work to complete, which was a review from the previous day. I knew it would be futile to give him that to do, so I stuck with a generic coloring activity.

I returned to my desk to wrap up attendance, lunch and ice cream orders, and await my first attempt in communication with Emanuel. I didn't have long to wait. I had been glancing over at him, smiling. He was a beautiful child. A head full of beautiful dark hair and dark eyes. He was of stocky build, a little above average in height for kindergarten, and very athletic looking. He would glance up at me shyly, smile, and return to his work. He seemed to be working diligently on his color sheet, carefully removing each crayon from the box and then returning it with great care. On my last glance at him, he kept his eyes locked on mine, then positioned his crayon to lie still on his sheet and stood up.

Oh, I thought. Here he comes, and all I know how to say is "taco."

He walked towards me, smiling. When he reached my desk, he cleared his throat and, in perfect English, asked, "May I go to the bathroom, please?"

I know my surprise surely registered on my face. "Of course, Emanuel," I answered, pointing to our bathroom door. "You just use the restroom, wash your hands afterwards, and come back to me so we can talk."

He nodded, smiled, and headed straight to take care of business.

In the meantime, my head was spinning. Could that sentence possibly be the only English he knew? Had someone thought to teach him that by sheer memorization? He was quickly right back to my desk. "Did you use the bathroom?" I inquired.

"Yes, ma'am," he answered politely, "and I washed my hands in the sink."

"Emanuel—" I began. "You speak English. Miss Wine told me that you didn't speak any English. How come no one knows you speak English?"

"Because no one speak English to me," was his matter-of-fact reply.

I had to sit back in my chair a moment and stare at this little prodigy in front of me. "Who taught you English?" I asked him.

"We live near a playground in Atlanta. I like to play basketball there. I learn English from my friends." He smiled. "I like to speak English."

"I can see you do," I answered. "And I can hear that you do it very well."

Emanuel grinned from ear to ear.

"Tell me, Emanuel. Does anyone in your family speak English?"

"No." He shook his head. "They only speak Spanish."

"So," I continued, "they only speak Spanish to you, so you only speak Spanish to them?"

He nodded. "They not learn how to speak English."

"When your aunt brought you to school this morning, did she talk to Miss Wine?"

"Yes." He nodded again. "She speak Spanish to my aunt, and she speak Spanish to me."

"Emanuel,"—I smiled and hugged him—"I am so happy you have come to our school and are in my class. You are going to love it here. And you will get to speak English to everyone, I promise, especially to me."

He smiled and returned to his desk.

All my worries of thirty minutes before dissipated into thin air. I couldn't wait for Miss Wine to return.

We were on our carpet for group time when Miss Wine appeared at my door. I met her in the doorway, and it was my turn to grin from ear to ear. "Miss Wine, I won't be needing you today," I said. "You underestimated my teaching skills."

She looked puzzled. "What do you mean?" she inquired.

"Well," I said boastfully. "I have managed to teach Emanuel perfect English in only thirty minutes."

She listened intently, amazed at my story. She was still shaking her head in disbelief as she left to attend to all the many students who *did* need her assistance.

So began my year with Emanuel. I am a firm believer in "things happen for a reason." Watching this child in my classroom was a lesson in resiliency and appreciation. He came from a meager household; although his clothes were clean each day, his outfits were few. Where other students went through two or three boxes of crayons, Emanuel never needed more than the one I gave him the day he arrived. He took the greatest care in keeping them nice. He was careful to never bear down hard and would return each to the box after using it.

Because he was away from his parents, my heart went out to him. His aunt lived in very crowded conditions with several families under one roof. I was never quite certain why Emanuel was sent to live with her, but I began to believe it was a safety concern. Where his family lived in Atlanta was a rough crime district.

I asked Miss Wine to speak to Emanuel's aunt to see if it would be permissible for me to take him on little outings with my children. She was very happy to grant permission. My children were the same age as Emanuel and got along fabulously. He often spent the entire weekend with us, attending church, fishing, and going out to eat at Mexican restaurants. His favorite was Chi-Chi's, and we were amazed at the hot sauce he poured on his food. He laughed that we couldn't handle the heat. His birthday came around, and he was so happy with the cake I made him. He said it was the first he had ever had.

A week before school was out, Emanuel was sent back to Georgia without ever getting to say goodbye. I received a handwritten note a month later from Emanuel's mother. A friend had written a translation for her. She wanted to thank me for all the care I had given him while she couldn't be with him.

I never saw Emanuel again but hope that wherever he was, he got to speak English, at least some of the time. I will forever remember how appreciative he was of things we so easily take for granted. I also no longer say, "I can't learn another language." I rephrase it now and say, "I'm too stubborn to learn, because I know I could if I really tried." I remember little Emanuel's face beaming when he gave me the surprise of a lifetime. "I like to speak English," he had said.

And I liked learning such a valuable lesson from my little fire-eating hot tamale!

Shayla

I was so fortunate to begin my teaching career at a small, isolated community elementary school. Tucked away on the top of a mountain, buses had to use every ounce of horsepower pulling their load up in the morning, then pray for solid brake pads in the afternoon as precious cargo was transported home. The teaching staff were a close, tightly woven community of our own. We felt we shared a common bond, teaching and protecting all the children who attended. We helped each other out, always on guard and ready to step in, if needed, whatever the crisis or situation.

Another unique feature of this little school was that it housed classes of every level of special education. We had the trainable mentally handicapped, the profoundly mentally handicapped, and the profoundly physically handicapped. I felt this offered and nurtured an acceptance among all the students for children of all degrees of mental and physical development. Just like the teachers, all the children at this little school shared a common bond.

Shayla was a twelve-year-old girl who was in the profoundly mentally handicapped class, even though she was being mainstreamed into the trainable class. Shayla had childhood disintegrative disorder, the most severe form of autistic-spectrum disorder. Her only form of communication was sign language, and her mastery of that had moved her into the trainable class, although her chances of ever being self-sufficient were slim to none.

We were all thrilled with Shayla's progress, and each morning her teacher walked her through the halls, working with her on her sign language. Almost animalistic in nature, Shayla's sense of smell was extremely keen. Whenever she met one of us, she pressed her nose in the location where her olfactory receptors drew her. This was how she identified people. I always wore my favorite perfume on my neck, and that was where Shayla's nose went. The secretary must have always had duplicating fluid on her hands, as Shayla gathered her hands and pressed her face into them. The PE teacher was greeted by Shayla with her nose pressed shoulder level at the armpits, so he always joked that his deodorant had to survive the "Shayla Test." You get the picture. Each time Shayla made a positive identification, she would excitedly confirm it—much like one does in charades—by patting the front of her face repeatedly with the palm of her hand.

We all adored Shayla. She added depth and meaning to our teaching profession, as did all the children in the special education classes. We learned, as with all children, that they were going to succeed and fail, exceed our expectations as well as our patience at times, and it was okay to laugh at the funny things they did—just like we laughed at the other children. It was all part of the developmental process. I thought it to be an extraordinary environment of acceptance and learning.

This particular day I was seated with my kindergarten class in the cafeteria, finishing up our lunch. We had a huge lunchroom, flanked by sunny windows, which were often opened wide to let in the gentle, mountain breeze. The special education classes had the same lunch schedule as we did, and they were seated on the opposite side of the room.

As I sat, reflecting on the afternoon schedule ahead, I casually took in my surroundings. I noticed the laughter of the children at a nearby table as they excitedly talked about their day. I noticed the lovely aroma of cinnamon buns being taken from the oven in preparation for the next day's breakfast. I noticed Mr. Prichard, our beloved janitor, leaning over the tray-return counter, amicably talking to one of our cafeteria staff. Yes, I certainly was fortunate to work in such a pleasant environment.

A child at my table needed help with a milk spill, so I was momentarily diverted from my daydreaming. Upon completion of this task, I returned to my seat. As my gaze once again returned to my happy surroundings, my eyes froze in horror. For there, at the tray-return counter, was Shayla, nose pressed up to the seat of Mr. Prichard's bib overalls, who was still leaned over, just resting his weary bones. She was excitedly sniffing and turning back to us, signing that she had made a positive ID.

I felt like I was in slow motion, but actually, I dashed across the room. Mr. Prichard, thank goodness, was oblivious to the commotion behind him as I gently placed my arm around Shayla and led her away. She continued her signing until I smiled and patted her shoulders, which was our affirmation of her successful identification. I walked her back to her teacher, and to my knowledge, I was the only one who had witnessed the incident.

Oh, Shayla, you taught me a valuable lesson. I became aware of how very important it is for all of us to surround ourselves with caring people who can watch that we don't make embarrassing social blunders. For we all make them, regardless of our mental capacities, and as I age, this becomes an even more important concern of mine.

Trent

I will never be a candidate to recruit for colleges or universities. I graduated from a wonderful university that started off as a teaching college; however, if anyone should ask me if what I learned at my four-year college of choice actually helped me on the job, I would have to answer no. I cannot think of one single, solitary thing, so I can't say that I'd do much for their college enrollment.

What I can say without a moment's hesitation that did help me were children like Trent, who, in their own way, taught me how to be a good teacher.

I had just been transferred to a very large elementary school. My first, smaller school, had been closed due to budget cuts. There were five classrooms for each grade, pre-k through fifth at my new school. Ironically, this was the same elementary school I had attended as a child.

The cafeteria was huge, and the room was lined with long, wooden tables with big, sturdy, wooden chairs. I was trying to fit in with the already established faculty and took my cues as to the routine of things by observation. I had always eaten with my students at my previous school, but I noticed a different pattern here. The children filled in at the lower end of the table, and the teachers all sat at the upper end of their individual row of tables. That way, I assume, they could all converse easily from one table to the next, even if it meant walking the few extra feet to talk to another teacher a few tables away. It was the "teachers' end" instead of a "teachers' table."

Not wanting to appear different, I followed example and sat at the head of the table with my entire class far away at the other end. That is . . . until Trent.

It was just the fourth week of school. Usually, new students don't start showing up until after Christmas, but Trent's father had taken a job with a local factory, so this was Trent's second school in just four weeks' time.

He had arrived that morning on the bus, so I hadn't even met his family. Such a cute kid: big, splotchy freckles, short, sandy hair, big ears, and a huge smile sporting two vacancies where front teeth had been. My favorite attribute was his slow, Southern drawl, which reminded me of Opie Taylor.

The morning went by quickly as I acclimated Trent to his new surroundings. I could tell he was used to moving around. He didn't seem to be at all frazzled by a new school, new classmates, or a new teacher.

Lunchtime arrived, and I led the class into the large, sunny room filled with the aroma of meatloaf and fresh pineapple cake. Anyone who has horrid memories come to mind of school food never ate in this cafeteria. The food was home cooked and delicious, and I watched as all the children settled into their chairs. Then I walked around, opening milk cartons and cutting up food. After I tended to all their needs, as well as their wants, I went through the line and got my tray, piled high with scrumptious hot food.

As I took my seat at the head of the table, I noticed Trent looking down the length of the table at me. He took a few bites of food, glanced at me, then ate a little more. This went on for a minute or two, with each glance looking a little more uneasy and restless. Then I saw him scoot his chair back, stand, pick up his tray, and start toward me. Next thing I knew, he was standing right beside me.

"Is this seat taken?" he asked me in that knee-deep, Southern drawl.

"No, Trent, it's not taken," I answered, a little confused.

"May I sit here?" he asked without hesitation.

"Of course," I answered, pulling the heavy wooden chair back for him.

As he sat down, he flashed that big, toothless grin, and his eyes reflected a mixture of friendliness and concern. "Mrs. Rodgers . . . do you got any friends?" he asked while glancing at all the empty seats close to me.

I had to smile. "Why, yes, Trent, I do have a couple of friends."

"That's good!" He smiled at that, looking relieved. Then he asked another question to start up our conversation. "Have you ever stepped in a cow dab?"

From that day on, I sat with my class at the other end of the table. Trent saw the distance between me and everyone else and took that to mean isolation. And to him, isolation meant loneliness. He was the new kid, but he was reaching out to me because he thought I needed a friend. Those are the kinds of things they don't teach you in college.

Stephanie

As a little girl, I entertained thoughts of several career choices. Because of my love for animals, I first thought of being a veterinarian. I scratched that when I heard of animals being "put down," "put to sleep," and "put out of their misery." Further research defined all of the above as meaning the animals were killed. Then, as a teenager, I joined some of my friends as a candy striper at the local hospital. I couldn't wait for the weekends. We would spend our Saturdays filling water pitchers, delivering and reading mail to patients, tending to them by changing their sheets, combing their hair, feeding them, and helping them dress. Working closely with all the medical staff was very inspiring. I wanted to be a nurse or even a doctor someday. The thought of saving lives seemed like a very noble calling. But then chemistry classes got the best of me. I didn't like them, didn't understand the periodic tables, and the thought of pursuing a career that required a weighted study in that subject area sent me in another direction. I loved children and they all seemed to love me. I began working in daycares part time and volunteering at summer camps. Yes, this felt right. I would be a teacher.

It would mean I was saving minds instead of lives, but still, it was a noble calling.

Then I learned, with Stephanie, that it was a calling that did both.

My second elementary school of employment was considered large by any standard. With five classrooms for each grade level, the student body totaled close to 750 students. We were fortunate to have each grade level clustered together. We helped each other in planning, teaching, and supervision.

My kindergarten classroom was at the end of the long hallway that ran the entire length of the ground level. I had one kindergarten class to my left, and the other three were the next doors up the hallway. I had a piano in my classroom, which I played daily. For thirty minutes each morning, I had two different kindergarten classes join me. They alternated days, and we all had a singing good time. I learned all eighty students' names that way, and everyone looked forward to coming to Mrs. Rodgers' class for music.

This little bit of background information is important to understand for the rest of my story. Even if a child was in another kindergarten classroom, I knew them personally because of my group music class.

Naptime was a cherished time at this school. The large windows were equipped with those heavy, pull-down shades, making the room very dark and restful. All of the children were worn out from their day of work and play, and they quickly fell asleep. It never took long for the snoring to start, making it a soothing background for the teachers to do their daily paperwork. That was precisely what I was doing this particular afternoon when the door was flung open and at least ten of the next-door kindergarten class came spilling into my room "Stephanie's choking!" they screamed.

I was across the room and out the door in probably one leap. In the hall I met my friend and co-worker holding little Stephanie, who was pale white and starting to turn blue around the lips. "She swallowed a marble, I think!" screamed her teacher. She passed her off to me and went running down the hall to call 911.

Stephanie was still conscious but fading fast. I could tell there was no air movement because of the terrifying silence. No gagging, no coughing. I had taken many CPR classes, which also included Heimlich training, and had been required to use it twice on both my children over the years. That was frightening enough, but this was someone else's baby girl, and her parents weren't here to help me. This was all on me.

I pulled Stephanie up to my chest, her back to me. Cupping my fists under her tiny rib cage, I began the familiar in and up thrusts. Over and over, I repeated my movements. Nothing. She went limp and her head and arms drooped down. I knew the time it would take to get EMS on the scene, and I knew this was critical. I had to make this work.

As Stephanie lost consciousness, I put everything I had into the last thrust. I knew it could mean crushing her ribs, but the alternative was worse. I felt the force all the way to my chest and at the same instant heard the glass marble hit the wall five feet away. Stephanie took in two large gasps of air and then began crying. We both slid to the floor in a pile. By then, her teacher was back on the scene. She lifted Stephanie from me and started back toward the office with her. EMS arrived and checked her over. She was fine, but her parents were called to take her home anyway.

As for me, the other kindergarten teachers watched my class while I went to the lounge to pull myself together. A cup of coffee and a comfy chair for five minutes and I was good as new.

The next day, Stephanie was back at school and greeted me in the hallway with a hug. "Thank you for getting the marble out of my throat," she said gratefully. "I thought I was going to see Jesus."

Stephanie, my little marble eater. She taught me that teaching isn't just about saving minds. These children are entrusted to us every day, and we must always be ready to also save their lives.

Bentley

Life is full of lessons. Some take years to learn and others just take seconds. Some come with tears attached, while others leave you rolling with laughter. And the lesson in some moments is that you don't really learn anything earth shattering from them except that it's okay to laugh hard or to cry hard. And the laughter or tears can hit you years later whenever you think of it. And you don't want to forget it—ever—simply because it makes you laugh or cry. I keep this memory for such a moment because I laughed so hard that I cried.

Every class seems to have a class clown. If the teacher is lucky, there is just one. It's the child who keeps something going all the time, purposely taking center stage to keep the laughs coming. It's usually a situation that requires teacher intervention to help the child corral this need for attention to appropriate times and settings; other-wise, your class environment would resemble a three-ring circus. I call this strategy, "Keeping it under the Big Top."

But what about the child who doesn't know they are funny? They do not crave the limelight. In fact, they are somewhat shy. They want to follow the rules, please the teacher, and keep a low profile. Yet, for whatever reason, *everything* they do is funny.

Bentley was a cute, cherub-like, little six-year-old. He had cheeks that you just wanted to tweak. His hair was kept in a neat little buzz cut, and one of his front teeth had been chipped at an angle that just gave him extra personality. He had already attended a private kindergarten but still needed another year to master a few more skills before entering first grade. I felt Bentley was just "a late bloomer." Developmentally, he was a good half year behind his classmates. His hand muscles were not fine-tuned yet, making it difficult to hold pencils or crayons. Yet they were soft and warm, perfect for holding hands. I was working with him on exercises that would strengthen his fine motor skills.

But the area that I couldn't help Bentley with, and the area in which he was most lacking, was just plain old common sense. And I suppose it was this undeveloped attribute that was the root of why he always kept everyone laughing. Everything he did, although unintentional, was absolutely hilarious.

It was always just little things, and reflecting on it, I suppose it was just the innocence on his little face that made each situation so funny. Like the time he called me over to the swing because it wasn't working.

"Teacher, it's broke," he lamented as he just sat still on the seat, watching all his classmates gleefully in orbit, soaring back and forth.

Or the time he was at the pencil sharpener an extra-long time. When I went to investigate, I found him trying to sharpen the eraser end. And on more than one occasion, I heard cries of "Help" coming from our bathroom. He would be trying to push the door open to get out, and he needed to simply pull it inward.

Sweet little Bentley. He had no idea how much I appreciated the levity he added to my day.

My favorite memory of all came on a day Bentley arrived a little late following a doctor's appointment. He had been given a required immunization shot, and it had left his rump feeling a little sore. After about two hours at school, he said he wasn't feeling well and wanted me to call his mommy. He didn't have a fever, but I was certain he was probably feeling discomfort. We walked down to the office after I secured someone to watch my class.

With Bentley standing right beside me, I called his mother. She was at work and really needed Bentley to stay at school if he wasn't really sick. She asked if she could speak to him. I was grateful for this because it meant I wouldn't have to make the judgment call. She could decide for herself. I handed Bentley the phone.

He dutifully took the phone and I stood close by, ready to take the receiver if she needed me again. I watched as sweet little Bentley held the phone to his ear. I couldn't help smiling at that innocent little face. I just adored him.

Then I saw him nodding his head as if he was answering yes to a question of hers. A few seconds later, he nodded again, a little more pronounced than before. It dawned on me what was happening.

"Bentley, your mommy can't see you," I calmly explained.

He looked up at me gratefully, as if he appreciated the information. Then he slowly held the receiver out at arm's length and raised it up a bit. He nodded yes again. Surely now his mommy could see him better.

Oh, my little Bentley. You taught me that all memories have a special purpose, and yours have always occupied a special place in my heart. It's that place that loves—and laughs—the hardest.

Kacey

Maybe I've always been a little partial to redheads. My son's first crush was on an adorable little red-haired girl down the street. My daughter had bright orange hair when she was born. And I have a gorgeous niece with long auburn locks.

So when the door to my room opened on registration day and a cute little redhaired charmer skipped into the room, I was thrilled. She had rosy cheeks, a few freckles, a big smile, and fiery red hair.

A young man was with her and also an older girl, probably around twelve years of age. She was tall and attractive, with blonde hair and model-like features. The man, who I assumed was Daddy, shook my hand and took a seat across from me. The girls eagerly set about giving the room a look-over.

He introduced himself and told me the two girls' first names, pointing them out individually across the room. As he watched me having difficulty finding the little one's name on my roster, he offered assistance. "Kacey's last name isn't the same as mine yet," he said.

While he spoke, he unfolded papers from his pocket and laid them on the table in front of me. They were legal documents granting him temporary custody of Kacey and her older sister. As all types of scenarios raced through my head, he began one that certainly hadn't crossed my mind.

He and Kacey's mother had only been married a short while when she was diagnosed with late-stage ovarian cancer, so advanced that surgery was not an option and treatment was futile. She had succumbed to the disease just three months before. He told me that in the short time she had left following the diagnosis, she had refused drugs that would have eased her pain but would have left her in a semi-conscious state. She wished to be able to communicate with her girls until the end. She had even purchased birthday cards and Christmas gifts for them to open from her up until their eighteenth birthdays.

As I heard this story, I pictured this beautiful, courageous woman, a mother and a newly wedded wife, facing her demise with no thought of herself, but rather of the family she was leaving behind. I drifted back to the voice of the young man across from me. Was I hearing correctly? Had he really said he would be adopting the two girls, and they would take his last name when the process was complete? How amazing! Here was a man choosing to carry on his late wife's legacy and raise her daughters alone.

At that point the two girls joined us at the table, happily telling their new daddy all about the classroom. Kacey even crawled up onto his lap. I chatted with Kacey briefly, letting her know what we would be doing the first day of school. She smiled excitedly at her daddy and me.

He hugged her and weighed his next words, since she was in such close proximity. "Things may be hard for a while, if you know what I mean. Just call me if you need me."

I promised I would, then watched as the two girls took his hand and left the room. That night I hugged my own babies and felt a rush of fear at the sheer thought of not seeing them grow up.

As the school year started, Kacey displayed a resiliency and strength that I'm certain reflected her mother's courageous battle. She was such a joy, always smiling, so well behaved, loved school, and was everyone's best friend. I was careful not to bring up the subject of her mother, but I stood by ready to allow her to talk if she wished. At least I thought I was ready.

The first time it happened, it snuck up on me, and emotionally, I saw I needed to buck up for Kacey's sake. We were cooking in the classroom, an activity I did every Thursday. All the children get to take part adding ingredients, and it's a fabulous learning experience for them.

As I was stirring the cake batter, Kacey left her seat around the oval table, came beside me, and placed her hand on top of mine as I held the spoon. She looked up at me with tear-filled eyes and said, "I always helped Mommy stir."

I was glad to have the help because my eyes blurred so badly I couldn't see the bowl.

Another day, not too long after this, the children were all sound asleep at rest time. I suddenly saw Kacey sit up on her mat, looking frantically around the room and then begin sobbing—no, wailing—head thrown back, tears streaming.

I rushed to her and picked her up, hugging her tightly to me. "What's wrong, Kacey? What happened?" I asked, patting her back and searching for whatever had hurt her.

"Mommy," she sobbed. "I dreamed Mommy was here and then I woke up and she's gone!"

We went to the rocking chair and spent the rest of the naptime rocking back and forth, back and forth.

Christmas came, and over the holidays, I thought of Kacey and her sister opening their gifts from their mama. I never heard anything about it when we returned to school, but I also didn't ask.

As the February snows melted, our thoughts turned to planting, and I began my study unit on spring. With my class seated on the carpet around me, I displayed pretty pictures of apple blossoms and tulips. Close by, I had my potting soil, cups, and seeds, ready for the children to get their hands dirty and plant a bean.

I was describing to a captivated audience how the seed bursts open in the soil when, suddenly, Kacey jumped to her feet, barely able to contain her excitement. "So it's spring? Right now, it's spring?" Her questioning eyes frantically searched mine for an affirmation.

"Why, yes, Kacey. It's spring. Is spring your favorite season?"

"Spring is when Mommy said my flowers would come up! We planted bulbs in the ground together, and she said they would come up in the spring. She said she would be in heaven when they came up, but the flowers would be her thinking of me. I need to see if they came up! Do you think she's thinking of me?"

Kacey was gone from my lesson at that point. My posters, my bean seed, and my potting soil all certainly paled in comparison to the far-off look and memory in her mind. She was once again with her mommy in the garden, planting together. As she scurried to her bus that afternoon, I prayed for a wonderful reunion in the flower patch, just Kacey and her beautiful, courageous mother.

Kacey, my brave little Kacey. Of all my students, I think she taught me most about what's important in life. Not only her, but also her mother and the only man she knows as Daddy. A man who stepped up to the plate when he didn't have to, a mother's love that defied death and still surrounded her daughters, and a little girl, a little red-headed girl who will forever be in my heart.

Maurice

Maurice was my Golden Boy. You know the ones— tall, lean, handsome features, with quick wit and an even quicker smile. Everything he did was perfect. He colored well and drew with exact detail. He quickly mastered the alphabet, and in between our lessons, crafts, and outdoor play, I easily taught him to read before any of the others had even shown an interest. Likewise, when it came to physical competition, he outran them all.

He had beautiful, tanned skin and almond-shaped amethyst eyes. I wondered about his family, as I only had contact with his mother through letters and phone calls. I was looking forward to our first parent-teacher conference after receiving a note that she would be able to attend.

At exactly six o'clock, Patricia Hagee walked in holding Maurice's and his younger brother's hands. Both children were dressed in fresh, clean clothes, different from what Maurice had worn that day. I thought this unusual, but refreshing, that a mother would take the time to clean up her child before bringing him back to school for a meeting. The other child was just as cute as Maurice and equally as well-mannered and pleasant. His mother was strikingly beautiful, a tall, statuesque woman with short, cropped hair and coffee-with-cream skin. I immediately saw the amethyst eyes and prominent bone structure that was shared by Maurice and his younger brother.

We exchanged pleasantries and sat down to go over Maurice's progress. She smiled and nodded and occasionally looked adoringly at Maurice and little Dillon. As I finished my review, Patricia spoke of how proud she was and then sent them both over to the toys across the room. I guessed this to be an effort to speak to me alone, and this proved to be correct. As soon as she saw her boys out of earshot and playing contentedly, she spoke. Her eyes locked on mine, and I saw such serenity and calm that I was unprepared for what followed. She told me her story.

As a young mother of two baby boys, her husband had beaten her repeatedly in front of them. He had finally been taken to jail and would be there for ten years, not only for assault but also for felony theft charges.

She had done all she could to see to it that her boys were taught right from wrong and prayed daily that they were too young to remember the beatings they had witnessed. She worked daily cleaning homes for people in the area and had even been fortunate enough to take on some businesses to clean at night. After she read to the boys and tucked them in, her sister would come and stay until she got back to the house in the morning. She was always, she emphasized, there to tuck them in herself and also to feed them breakfast and get them off to school and daycare before she began her long, strenuous workday.

Closing the conference, she asked me for a copy of the Dolch reading word list for first grade, as she was also working with Maurice on his reading and wanted him to be prepared for the next year. She was the only parent who made that request. As she exited the room, I watched her holding her sons' hands, smiling and chatting happily with them. It painted such a contrast to what the picture of this family could have been if not for this strong, beautiful, devoted mother.

As the school year progressed so did the deterioration of my own personal life. I recall one morning after leaving a particularly chaotic scene. I was wearing dark glasses to hide tear-swollen eyes. As I led the class out to the playground for a few minutes of recess to get myself composed, Maurice ran up beside me. As I looked down at him, he flashed that winning smile as he asked in his usual mannerly style, "Mrs. Rodgers, may I hold your hand?"

Choking back the sobs that had been ready to burst out all morning, I answered, "Yes, Maurice, you can. There's no one else holding my hand right now."

"Well, that's just not right," he replied, slipping his little hand into mine and squeezing tightly. "All girls need to have their hands held."

What a lesson from my little Golden Boy. We should always keep watch. There may be someone around us who needs a touch, a hug, or to simply have their hand held. It will make a difference.

Bobbie Jo

There's one in every crowd . . . and during this school year, it was Bobbie Jo. The one who tries to make truth out of every mistruth if it will benefit them. They usually succeed because they are just so adorable. God blessed them with cute, physical attributes. In Bobbie Jo's case, it was dimples settled like craters on either side of a wide, flashing smile absent of two front teeth. She was a well-nourished child, sporting dimples in other places as well. Just adorable.

What is equally dangerous with these children and, later as adults, is that they use this cuteness to camouflage their sneakiness and, ultimately, their lies. It is a challenge to anyone around them to accomplish the task of breaking their bad habits before adulthood.

One afternoon during our usually serene rest time, I was busy doing paperwork at my desk. The light filtering in around the drawn shades gave just enough light for me to monitor the sleeping children and focus on my deskwork. I abruptly became aware of a disturbance in the far corner of the room. Little Julianna suddenly jumped up from her mat and came running to me, shedding tears that were literally leaping from her eyes. "Bobbie Jo has my lipstick," she wailed, throwing herself into my arms.

"What lipstick," I asked. "Did you bring lipstick to school today?"

She was sobbing so hard that all she could do was nod her head. After reminding her that bringing lipstick to school was not allowed, I set about to get the issue solved. "Bobbie Jo," I called in a voice loud enough for her to hear but not awaken the others. "Do you have Julianna's lipstick?"

"No, I don't," she shot back. "Julianna's *lying*."

"Are you certain?" I asked. "Julianna is upset, and she says you do have her lipstick."

"*I do not*," Bobbie Jo stated emphatically, her back still turned away from me as she lay on her rest mat.

I looked at Julianna. Tears still streaming, she managed to speak. "Mrs. Rodgers, Bobbie Jo *does* have my lipstick."

I so wanted to believe there had been a big mistake. "Bobbie Jo, please come here. Julianna still says you have her lipstick."

At that point Bobbie Jo sat up on her mat in the far corner of the room, and in a voice that was a mixture of sticky sweetness and subtle sneakiness, she retorted, "I do not!"

The afternoon light filtering in around the drawn

shades illuminated the truth. For around Bobbie Jo's lips and smeared into those creviced dimples was the brightest, reddest lipstick I had ever seen. In my Grandmother's words, "Those lips resembled a hen's a$$ at pokeberry time."

During the following years, I was to teach—and meet as adults—many Bobbie Jos. Often their mistruths weren't as easy to read as those red lips. But she taught me that I still had to remember that *all* lips can be deceiving, even the adorable ones.

Makayla Rose

Everyone is familiar with the idiom "cusses like a sailor." And usually, the mental picture it conjures up for me is of a burly, stubbly bearded, pot-bellied roughneck. That was before. Before I met Makayla Rose.

I well remember the day I met her. My assistant had set up a desk in the foyer of our school, and parents brought their little ones by to register for the pre-school test required by the county. I usually didn't meet the candidates that day. That was done on the actual testing day. But my assistant could not resist this one. She stuck her head in my classroom and asked if I could meet someone. I motioned her in.

The door opened and I saw a young woman walk in. But all I saw of the little one with her was the top of a head walking past the low bookshelf in front of me. I stood up and laid eyes on the tiniest child I had ever seen proclaiming to be of preschool age. She was so small. Perfectly formed but the height that children are usually measured in inches—not feet. I stood in front of her, introduced myself to her mother, and then turned my attention to Makayla.

"Why, hello to you," I said, smiling at the sweetest little face I had ever seen.

Her blue eyes were like quarter-sized buttons, and all her other features had to be tiny in order to make room for them on her face. Her hair was a mix of various blondes and fell like cornsilk around her shoulders. She looked just like Cindy Lou Who from Dr. Seuss' *How the Grinch Stole Christmas.* I squatted down so I could look straight into her face. What she did and said next will forever bring tears to my eyes whenever I recall it.

Makayla looked up at her mother, and then taking in a full breath of air, as if she were mustering up the courage to go into battle, she took one step toward me. And in her little Cindy Lou Who voice, she asked, "Will you hurt me?"

I melted. I reached both arms around her and pulled her close. "Of course not, sweetie," I said. "And I won't let anyone else hurt you either."

"Okay," she said meekly.

And so began my year with Makayla Rose. I had made a pact with her, and I was going to honor it somehow. Somehow, this wisp of a child was going to have to maneuver through halls, on buses, and on playgrounds while everyone towered above her. It turned out to be a task that wasn't as difficult as it seemed. I had underestimated the feisty spirit of Makayla Rose.

The first day of school, in my opinion, has to be the best day, the most exciting one, especially in pre-k. You have one chance to hook them, just like a trophy catfish.

You want them to love school, to always want to come back, no matter if its rain, hail, sleet or snow—or even homesickness.

I always do my Gingerbread Man on the first day. I read the story to the children, we learn the chant, and then we cut one out of brown construction paper, paste on black eyes and buttons, and make a mouth out of red dots. Then comes the best part. We pop him in my magic oven—constructed from a brown cardboard box made to resemble a kitchen stove. Unbeknownst to the children, I had prebaked a *real* gingerbread man and had him tucked secretly inside. After we wave a magic wand over the oven, and the children each come up and chant their magic words, we take a whiff. Ooh! Can you smell him baking? Naturally, they all can. Then I reach in and voila! I pull out the real gingerbread man to all the excited oohs, ahhs, and squeals from the children.

At that point I have set the stage for the kids, for myself, and for their entire school year. The kids can now perform magic, I am magic, and their preschool year is going to be magical. I just love it!

But that is not the end of the lesson. Just like the story, the gingerbread man must now run away. So I have already prearranged for the school nurse to come by and steal him while I have all the children out of the room on the playground. She hides him in the principal's office, thus beginning the chase.

We return to the room, and upon discovering that the gingerbread man is missing in action, we begin our search. This is the purpose of the whole lesson. It's my way of taking these little ones on a grand tour of their school and introducing them to each of the new adults in their lives. We head to the library, the cafeteria, the gym, the clinic, and finally end up in the principal's office where he, or she, relates to the children how the gingerbread man was caught running down the hall and brought into the office. I also add that *everyone* caught running in the halls gets taken to the principal's office.

We proudly walk back to our classroom, carrying our captured man, and devour him with milk before he has the opportunity to run away again.

Well, back to Makayla Rose. She bounced with excitement the entire morning. She told and retold all the events to her classmates, although they had all seen it firsthand. When my friend and fellow teacher walked into the room to hand me a memo, Makayla ran to share the news with a new person. "The gingerbread man RAN AWAY!" she squealed.

"What?" asked my friend, smiling at this tiny little person.

"I said, "THE GINGERBREAD MAN RAN AWAY!" Makayla repeated.

My friend was so intrigued, as well as smitten, by this little cherub of a person that she knelt down at eye level in order to get all the facts. "Tell me what happened," she implored.

Makayla eagerly retold the entire morning's events, eyes wide with excitement, waving her hands dramatically to emphasize the grand jump down from the high countertop where we had placed him.

"So the gingerbread man jumped down," my friend reiterated. "And tell me, what did he do then?"

"Well," Makayla said, blue eyes still open wide with excitement. "He hauled ass, I guess."

My friend fell backwards on the floor, it caught her so off guard. The wad of chewing gum she secretly had in her mouth shot out, and I gasped, looking quickly around to see how many children, on their first day of school, had just heard profanity.

My friend, stifling her snickers that turned into full-fledged belly laughing as soon as she left my room, went dashing to tell everyone in the teachers' lounge.

I drew in a labored breath and pulled Makayla to me as I sat down in the nearest chair. Looking at that innocent little face, I could easily tell she had no idea what had just happened. "Makayla," I began. "I am so happy that you enjoyed the gingerbread man so much that you wanted to share the story, but there is a word that you used that you can't say here at school."

Again, the innocence in her eyes let me know she hadn't a clue.

You can't say, 'hauled ass.' You must say 'ran fast' or 'ran quickly' or something like that. Do you understand?

'Ass' is a bad word. We all get in trouble if we use that word, even me. Do you understand?"

She nodded that she did, and in the days, weeks, and months that followed, she proved that she did indeed understand, for never again did I hear the word "ass." However, one by one, I had the task of eliminating quite a repertoire of profane words from Makayla's vocabulary.

Snack day arrived. This is the treasured day when each child gets to provide snacks for the entire class, pass them out, and hear the whole group in unison say, "Thank you." Makayla loved Fig Newtons and had carefully placed two on each child's napkin. She noticed that Blake and Peter hadn't touched theirs nor had they thanked her. She inquired why they weren't eating them.

"We don't like them," was Blake's reply.

"Well." Makayla shrugged as she turned back to her Fig Newtons. "Ya'll are just a bunch of bastards."

I put my hand on Makayla's shoulder and whispered in her ear. She nodded. "Bastard" was now eliminated.

At lunchtime each day, Makayla had to sit in a highchair beside me because she was too small to sit on the benches at our pre-k table. She had a voracious appetite, loved all types of vegetables and pastas, and usually ate everything on her lunch tray. She always inquired about my packed lunches, which were normally just leftovers from the evening before. On occasion, I even shared with her.

One day, as I ate my homemade spaghetti, Makayla looked over at it, interested. "What's that?" she inquired, putting her finger right on a carrot shred.

"That's a carrot," I answered, wiping off her finger with my napkin.

"Oh," she asked, finger back in my spaghetti, touching a mushroom, "And what's that?"

"That's a mushroom," I answered, once again wiping her finger.

Knowing that I had several more vegetables that her finger would probably seek out, I went ahead and told her all the wonderful ingredients I put in my spaghetti sauce.

"Oh," she smiled, nodding approval. "That be bitching!"

Throughout the year, one by one, I helped Makayla clean up her vocabulary. There was an "Oh, Hell!" when someone turned the light off on her when she was in the bathroom and an "Oh, shit!" when a fire drill interrupted center time. Each word was never, ever repeated once she knew it was a "bad word."

During science one day, I was doing my unit on snakes, and the class was intrigued by all the pictures and books and snakeskins I had on display. As I read a Big Book on snakes to the class, I turned a page to show a python swallowing a gazelle. All the children gasped, and some of the little boys yelled, "Cool!" But I noticed little Makayla just stared at the picture. She sat motionless and expressionless throughout the remainder of the lesson.

As we broke for centers, each child had their choice of which station to work or play in. I also left out the materials used in the science lesson so the children could revisit them if they so desired. I noticed Makayla slowly rise and head over to the Big Book about snakes. All the other children had scurried to the kitchen, or to the blocks, or to painting, or to dramatic play. Makayla was alone on the carpet, standing in front of the easel holding the snake book. She carefully turned the pages until the image of the snake swallowing the gazelle came into view. I watched her from some distance away. She had no idea that she had an audience of one. I saw her eyes resting on the cruel picture, and then I saw her draw in a deep breath and let it out in a slow sigh. "Damn snake," she whispered.

I let Makayla keep that one. I agreed! It was a damn snake.

Makayla moved away after that year, and I never saw her again. What I learned from her is that we as teachers have to patiently understand that our children come from environments that we can't control. Her use of profanity was not in her DNA. Someone, somewhere, had influenced her speech, although I never knew who it was, and it also didn't matter. With love and patience, I tamed her tongue, and in the process, I learned "feisty" goes a long way out in the world.

Jamarr

There was absolutely nothing written beside the student's name that indicated anything out of the ordinary. Nor did I know that the little boy who was about to enter my classroom door was far from ordinary. Unbeknownst to me, I was going to laugh more, cry more, and learn more about the human spirit than ever before. At that moment I had no idea that I was about to meet a child who would change my life forever.

It was registration day for kindergarten. I had been in my classroom since 8:00 a.m. and had met all my students except one. Looking at the clock on the wall, I saw that it was 4:30, and I would be leaving in thirty minutes. Hopefully, the family would come in soon. I do like to meet all the children and get necessary paperwork out of the way.

Just then, there was movement in the doorway. I looked over to see the widest grin I had ever seen. A little face was peeping around the door. I heard a woman say, "Go on in, Jamarr. Go in and meet your teacher."

The smiling face entered and my breath caught in my throat as I got a full visual on what he brought with him.

He walked in a limping gait as he dragged an enormous leg behind him with each step. He kept smiling at me as he walked straight to the toys I had set out to occupy the children as I met with the parents.

His mother flashed an equally captivating smile. She greeted me warmly and took the seat in front of me. Her name was Mornet, she said, and she introduced Jamarr and his brother. She then drew in a long breath and began her story.

Jamarr was to have been a conjoined twin. His brother died in the womb and Jamarr absorbed the body. His left side was affected. As Jamarr grew, the cells of his brother continued to grow, and, since birth, every six months he had to undergo painful surgeries. The doctors had to remove as much of the rapidly growing cells as possible. His left leg was basically the size and weight of another child. His feet were clubbed with extra toes. This made finding shoes and walking a great challenge. I noticed he wore black leather shoes with a red Nike Swoosh on the sides. The left shoe was at least twice the size of the right one. His mother explained that the shoes were custom made and a gift from Michael Jordan. The basketball star had heard of Jamarr through hospital staff and had kept him in shoes since he began walking.

Tears formed in my eyes as this devoted mother told me of all the surgeries, the times when she had almost lost him, and her fears for him as he began school. As she spoke, I stole glances at Jamarr across the room. He was always ready with that bright smile. I instantly loved him.

His mother explained that, more than anything, she wanted Jamarr to have a normal life. She said she knew there would be stares, and questions, and challenges. Jamarr was ready to face all of them. She told me of a time recently in a grocery store when Jamarr saw a few adults staring at him. He had calmly approached them and said, "If you want to know about my leg, just ask me. I will tell you. But please don't stare at me."

She told me about the sores that often developed on his leg around his shoes. The fluid built up and caused swelling. When that happened, it is very painful for him to walk. She also gave me the date of his next surgery, adding that he would miss a week or two of school. As she was completing Jamarr's paperwork, I became aware of someone standing behind me. I turned to see Jamarr inches away, just flashing that beautiful smile.

"Are you excited about coming to school?" I asked.

He nodded, still smiling. Then I saw him brace himself with his hands as he momentarily lost his balance. I could tell that the extra weight on one side of his body kept him always leaning slightly.

I watched as the family exited the room. Jamarr paused at the door, turned back, and waved at me. I smiled and waved at the little boy who in just thirty minutes had entered my classroom—and my heart.

The first day of school began pretty much the same as any other year. There were a few tears from one or two children but none from Jamarr. He had boarded the school bus and walked the entire distance from the bus-unloading platform unaided. That was probably the length of an entire football field, in addition to climbing a flight of stairs. He had to have been utterly exhausted. In order to walk, he basically just stepped ahead with his right foot and then dragged his left leg. It was very slow going.

I immediately set about adjusting our schedule to allow for the extra time it would take for us to get to gym class, the library, to lunch, and to the buses.

Earlier, I'd had what I thought to be a wonderful idea. That morning before the buses arrived, I had called Central Office and asked how I could obtain a wheelchair for Jamarr to use when he tired of walking. My "light-bulb" idea had been shot down. I was told it was the family's responsibility, not the school system's, to provide a wheelchair for Jamarr. I was heartbroken and disheartened. Jamarr's family was strapped with medical bills. They could not purchase a wheelchair for him.

As the morning progressed, I saw one of Mornet's fears dissipating. Children are so accepting and loving. Not one single child seemed afraid of Jamarr's appearance. He was just one of them, and my new little class quickly bonded. Everything was going to be all right.

But then the unexpected happened. The alarm sounded for a fire drill on the very first day of school. I had not progressed far enough with my planning for the year to have figured this one out. I quickly gathered my class in a line and told them to follow me. Then I looked at Jamarr and the realization hit me. He would never be able to get out in under a minute by walking. I saw a very simple solution. Squatting in front of Jamarr with my back to him, I said, "Jamarr! Wrap your arms around my neck." He quickly obeyed.

The confusion of the fire alarm and flashing lights had all the children somewhat frightened. As soon as I felt his hands clasp in front of me, I hoisted him on my back and stood. His full weight stunned me. His left leg alone felt like it weighed sixty pounds. I briefly told the children what was going on and we headed toward our exit. As we approached the door, at what I considered to be a speedy pace, Jamarr whispered in my ear, "Can't you go any faster?" After saying that, I heard him giggling.

That was the first of countless piggyback rides. We saved that means of transportation for emergencies or when Jamarr simply became exhausted. Just experiencing his weight for short periods of time gave me an idea what it was like for him *all* the time. Once I asked Jamarr if he was tired from walking. His response surprised me and brought to mind a favorite song of mine. Smiling, he looked at his leg and answered, "He ain't heavy. He's my brother."

He never complained . . . about anything. There were times when I would see him wincing as he walked. I would check his leg and find sores from his shoes. He quickly felt comfortable enough with me to allow me to remove his shoes and treat the sores. I would fashion a soft padding from gauze and replace the shoe. His eyes and smile would reflect his gratitude.

All the children in my class loved Jamarr, and he loved them. He was so sensitive to everyone's feelings and was always the one trying to cheer others up.

One morning, little Kendra came to school, crying. She and her brother had squabbled at home and she was still upset. She went into our walk-in coatroom and sat on the bench, crying softly, so I went in to talk to her. As we chatted, Jamarr slowly walked into the coatroom and got his book bag down. I thought he was just looking for ice cream money or something as he stuck his entire face down into his bag. Then he brought his head back up, sporting the Groucho Marx glasses, nose, and mustache I had given to all the children on Halloween. Little Kendra forgot all about her tears and gave way to full belly laughter. Jamarr waited until he was certain she was all better, then he took off the mask and put it back in his book bag.

Sometime around Christmas, Jamarr was hospitalized for another surgery to remove the growing cells of the twin he had never met. The incision would stretch down his entire left side. We missed him terribly, and the children made cards and drew pictures to decorate his room.

When he arrived back at school, I had a surprise waiting for him. An employee from the local Office Supply had seen me carrying Jamarr on my back sometime before Christmas. He had generously donated a wheel-chair for me to push Jamarr in at the school.

I painted a handmade license plate that read "Jamarr's Cadillac," and he proudly took his first ride to the play-ground. I allowed the children to take turns being his driver. He really liked his new ride, but we still did piggy-back occasionally just for old times' sake.

Our Field Day was fast approaching, and all the chil-dren were eagerly awaiting their race assignments. There was a huge competition among the classrooms as to who would win the trophy for each grade level. As we headed to the playground to begin practice, my heart turned to Jamarr. I had to come up with a way he could participate. I remembered his mother telling me that, as a toddler, Jamarr rolled on the floor instead of crawling. I immedi-ately had one of those "lightbulb" ideas.

I approached our PE teacher about adding a Log Roll Race to the list of Field Day events. One child from each of the five kindergarten classes would roll from the start line across the field—about twenty-five feet—to the finish line. My fondest memory of that Field Day is of Jamarr rolling across the finish line yards ahead of the others to win the blue ribbon.

As the school year entered the final month, I began my unit on careers titled "What I want to do when I grow up." With my class seated on the carpet all around me, each child in turn told their dream. One wanted to be a fireman, another a policeman. There was a teacher, a doctor, a cheerleader, and a baseball player. When it was Jamarr's turn, he got a faraway, wistful look in his eyes and said, "I want to run."

I had to choke back tears. Being a runner myself, I thought what I did daily without even thinking about it was something this little boy wanted more than anything else in the world. It was his life dream. Again, I just knew I had to do something. I called Jamarr's mother that afternoon and told her my plan. The following weekend, I was scheduled to run in a 5-K race. With her permission, I planned to push Jamarr in a racing stroller.

On the morning of the race, Jamarr was so excited. We each had our number taped to our shirts. I fastened a sign to the back of the stroller with my favorite Bible verse, Isaiah 40:31: "But those who hope in the Lord will renew their strength. They will mount up on wings like eagles; they will run and not grow weary. They will walk and not faint."

When the starting gun fired, we were off. The route was hilly, and as we headed on the downside of the first one, Jamarr spread his arms wide. He was jubilant, feeling the breeze rushing by his face. No words passed between us over the course of the race, but the unspoken communication will forever be treasured. We passed over the finish line, each winning first place in our own age division. Jamarr proudly wore his medal to school the following Monday.

During the last two weeks of school, Jamarr's mother came to see me. From the look on her face, I knew something was gravely wrong. Jamarr's last doctor visit had not gone well. The surgeries designed to relieve some of the weight from Jamarr's spine were no longer effective. The cells were growing more rapidly, and the pull on his spine would eventually paralyze him. The decision had been made to remove his leg.

I was there when they wheeled Jamarr back to his room following the surgery. I had an Etch-A-Sketch, puzzles, books, and donuts—some of life's little necessities.

He looked so small in the huge hospital bed. Without his leg, he was the size of any other five-year-old. Already sitting up, he flashed that winning smile.

Jamarr's father was a stocky, towering hulk of a man. Unable to handle the stress of the hospital waiting room, he had been walking the halls. He entered the room and went to stand at the foot of Jamarr's bed. His eyes fell on the plastic surgical wraps mounded where Jamarr's leg had once been. Tears streamed down his face.

Jamarr had been fiddling with his new Etch-A-Sketch but laid it down and looked at his father. I can still hear his consoling words. "Don't cry, Daddy," he said softly. "I love my new leg."

I think everyone in that room was somehow forever changed at that moment. Jamarr's new leg was no leg at all. He had dragged an enormous weight all his short life, and now he was set free.

Oh, Jamarr, my always smiling, precious gift from God. You taught me that miracles are a very real part of life. And these miracles can present themselves to us in many ways and in unsuspecting forms. My greatest miracle came to me in the life and spirit of an extraordinary little boy. A little boy who urged everyone around him not to cry. A little boy who faced obstacles with a smile. A little boy who carried the weight of his brother and never complained. A little boy who taught me to appreciate the little things in life that somehow get taken for granted.

A little boy who, in an instant, found the pathway to my heart . . . and forever stayed there.

Samantha

She looked like a porcelain doll. With golden-brown hair in perfect ringlets around shoulders that were flanked in lace. You could just tell this family had always wanted a little girl.

Her name was Samantha, and as soon as I saw her, I knew I would have to keep my room squeaky clean. I felt that if dirt touched her little body, she might dissolve. Her clothes were picture perfect, and every day she looked like she was dressed for a model shoot.

She was a perfectionist in her work and always made certain that every paper was neat and correct. She headed to the kitchen at center time and set right to housekeeping, dressing the dolls and setting the table. I didn't think I had ever seen such a girly girl. Wearing Sunday shoes almost every day, her playtime usually involved just skipping around and maybe getting on the swings occasionally. Her mother had never sent tennis shoes, so I assumed she didn't want Samantha soiling her clothes or climbing on the equipment and possibly bruising that flawless skin.

Spring rolled around and the memo went out for Field

Day. At our particular elementary school, Field Day was a super big event. Competition between the classes was high and trophies were awarded at each grade level. Being a runner myself, I had that competitive edge. I liked winning.

By this time I had seen all the children in action and was confident I knew which event each child would excel in. I put my fastest runners in the 50-yard dash and the 200-yard stick relay. My physically slower children were put in the egg race, three-legged race, and the sack race. We had a new event called the Shoe Scramble, when children had to race barefoot, put on shoes, tie them up, and race back. I wasn't sure who to put in that one, as we had not yet mastered shoe tying.

On our first day of practice, I had everyone in their scheduled events. I had placed Samantha in the egg race because all it required was balancing an egg on a spoon and basically walking faster than anyone. I felt Samantha could do that well, as she had such superb poise and composure. I was correct. She walked quickly with ease and grace, even extending her pinkie finger in the air while holding that spoon.

On the second day of practice, I was feeling fairly good about our chances at beating out the other kindergarten classes in just about every event. However, my 50-yard dashers were a tad sluggish, and I looked around to find a replacement. I asked several of my fastest runners if they wanted to switch assigned races.

At that point, Samantha came to me. "Mrs. Rodgers, may I run in the race?" she asked sweetly, twirling a ringlet around her finger.

I looked down at her perfectly appointed outfit and shiny black patent leather shoes. Thankfully, that would be my excuse to refuse. "Why, I'm sorry, Samantha, but you don't have any running shoes on."

"But I can run without my shoes on," she replied sweetly, batting long eyelashes and smiling coyly.

I started to refuse again, possibly voicing the danger of running shoeless. But the new Shoe Scramble race made that a useless argument. "Well, okay, Samantha. I'll let you try the race and see how you do, but you are my Number One best egg racer and I would hate to lose you." I smiled to myself at what a great excuse that would be after this botched attempt of hers.

So I pulled all my 200-yard relayers and my 50-yard dashers to the starting line, as well as my now shoeless little Samantha.

"On your mark, get set, GO!" I yelled.

What happened next is what only happens at the Olympics or the Kentucky Derby. Samantha flat left everyone yards and yards behind as a whirl of curls and lace crossed the finish line while everyone else was at midfield. I was still standing, mouth open, as she turned and ran back to me.

"Mrs. Rodgers, did I do good?"

My little Golden Girl Samantha. She taught me to *always* dig a little deeper and find all those hidden talents. *All* children have them.

Dovie

She always wore her hair in five perfect braids, tied off at the ends with big, colorful, ball elastic bands. The colors of the bands changed daily, but the braids never did; always five and always in the same places. But that's the only thing that stayed the same about Dovie. She was in constant motion, flitting here and there, and full of energy. One of the tiniest children in my class but with the biggest personality. Her mother worried that she might be "slow" because, in her opinion, Dovie couldn't understand things. I didn't see a problem. I think Dovie was so smart that she knew how to "work" her mama. Dovie was indeed lazy when it came to doing things she wasn't interested in. So, I guess if one pretends they don't know how to do something, it's understandable that it won't get done. Nor will anyone force you to do it.

But in my classroom Dovie didn't attempt the power struggle. She did what I wanted because that was the only way she could do what *she* wanted. Dovie was not mentally challenged or slow, and she fully understood things. She had insight well beyond her young years.

About the time I was teaching Dovie, my personal life was falling apart. This book is not about that, so I won't veer off the path and dwell on it. However, in order to continue about Dovie, I have to set the stage.

One morning, I arrived at school exhausted and physically drained. Basically, I was very sad. I did my job that day, but I was definitely not myself. Dark glasses hid my tear-swollen eyes.

Recess came around, and I led the children out to the playground while another child went to get the ice cream order. I sat down on a bench to watch the children at play. When the ice cream order arrived, I passed them out, Dovie getting her usual Mickey Mouse bar—vanilla ice cream with two chocolate ears. She climbed up on the bench beside me like she always did. Often, she would hand the ears to me to eat because she didn't like chocolate. I tried to persuade her to just get vanilla ice cream, but she said, "No thank you. I like to share with you."

As she opened her ice cream, I noticed she kept glancing over at me, studying me carefully. After about two minutes of this, she finally spoke. "Mrs. Rodgers, do you have a husband?"

Surprised at the question, I simply replied, "No, Dovie. I don't really have a husband."

That satisfied her for only mere seconds.

"Mrs. Rodgers, do you have a boyfriend?"

Feeling strangely vulnerable now, I drew a deep breath

and answered her, "No, Dovie. I don't have one of those, either."

At that, I watched Dovie lay her ice cream carefully down on the wrapper. She then climbed over into my lap and, facing me, took my sunglasses off my face and laid them down beside me. Dovie then put her tiny hands on either side of my face and looked right into my eyes, holding me firmly so I couldn't turn away. I was barely breathing as she studied my face. It felt like she was looking into my soul.

"Mrs. Rodgers, why don't anybody love you?"

The shock was as if someone had slapped me. Not to alarm Dovie as to the impact her words had on me, I hugged her tightly, then picked her up and sat her down on the bench. Seizing my sunglasses quickly to hide the tears that by now were filling my eyes, I walked over to where some other children were playing on the jungle gym.

Still reeling from the intuitive accuracy of Dovie's questions, my mind raced over the morning's activities, trying to determine what had given me away. I could think of nothing I had said or done except that I had probably been noticeably "out of character," unhappy, even sad in my body language.

Then my thoughts turned to Dovie. In her world, and in the short four years of her life, she had learned to eat, speak a language, stand upright and walk, even run, had mastered playing and laughing, toilet training, and dressing herself. And also, in this short little life of hers, she had noticed the people around her and the emotional pain of those she cared about. She had surmised that people were sad if they didn't have someone who loved them.

Dovie was not "slow." She had already developed an insight many adults never nurture. I will never forget her or the impact I felt when another person, even one so young, saw through the careful camouflage and addressed my pain. She forced me to realize the situation and, because of that, to eventually do something about it.

April

Before I introduce April, I must first have you meet her older brother, Armando. He is how I became acquainted with the Garcia family.

It was midyear. My kindergarten class was well into their routine, and I had everyone where they needed to be skill-wise. This elementary school was nestled in the heart of a factory town. We were just beginning to see a growing population of immigrants moving here for employment. I had previously had experience from one other child from Mexico, and he had spoken fluent English. So when the secretary met me at lunch with a new student, I wasn't particularly concerned. He was Hispanic, but I guessed that he too probably spoke English as well.

It only took a minute to have this perception dissipate into thin air. We were already in the lunch line, so I needed to get him fed before I began the process of assessment. I asked him if he was hungry and he just stared at me, smiling. He hadn't a clue as to what I had said, but he seemed to like the way I said it. He was absolutely adorable! So short, with dark hair, dark eyes, and amaretto skin. He seemed to be smiling all the time.

I was amazed that he appeared to be comfortable, unafraid, and perfectly content to be in a school full of strangers with whom he could not communicate.

I positioned him in line behind one of my little girls. You know the old adage, "when in Rome . . . " I hoped he could just observe the others and do as they did. As I watched him, I noticed him eying the little girl, looking her up and down. Her back was to him, so she was oblivious to all the visual attention being given her by this tiny admirer. After moving his eyes up and down from head to toe maybe twice, Armando smiled and patted her bottom.

I immediately guided him to the back of the line . . .behind a boy.

A couple of weeks passed before I met the rest of the Garcia family. There was an older brother, age eight, and a beautiful sister, April, age two. The daddy spoke very good English, and Irma, the mother, was learning. She could get by. I took an instant liking to her. She was so industrious. When she came to the classroom to discuss Armando's progress, she challenged me to allow her to teach me Spanish if I would teach her English. It was an arrangement that led me to her home one night a week.

They had a small trailer, kept as neat as a pin. I noticed the furniture was worn and needed recovering, so I offered her a bolt of upholstery material I had left over from a project. With only a needle and thread, she covered an entire couch and chair to perfection.

At some point during the school year, Irma discovered she had another baby on the way. However, there was something terribly wrong with the way she was feeling. With the nearest high-risk clinic an hour away, and the Garcia family not owning a car, she needed transportation. I began taking her to her appointments once a week and ended up being with her when she went into labor during one of those trips to the doctor. When the little girl was successfully delivered, Irma named her Misty Elizabeth. I felt very honored because Betsy is a common nickname for Elizabeth.

Armando finished up his kindergarten year, learning English and mastering skills quickly. During the two years before April was ready to start school, she became fluent in English and Spanish. I was thrilled to have my own in-house interpreter, as I had six Hispanic children in my classroom that year. (We only had one ESL teacher and she had over seventy-five students school-wide.) With the exception of April, all spoke Spanish only. Yet I didn't feel the helplessness I had felt in previous years. With April readily available, things were going to run much smoother and incredibly easier. Selfishly, I never stopped and thought of the pressure I was putting on sweet little April.

It is amazing how fast children can assimilate language. I had been open-minded and eager to learn Spanish from April's mother, but so far I was still a struggling student. Watching April move about the classroom and interpreting directions for the other children was nothing short of astounding. When she was translating for the other children, I would hear her emphasizing the English nouns first, then the verbs. Unknowingly, she was teaching a language, and her students were learning quickly.

It became such a predictable part of my schedule, sending April about the room to check understanding, that I didn't give it appropriate thought—until the meltdown.

One of my Spanish students was quite unruly. He wasn't picking up English as quickly as the others, and I was beginning to think it was on purpose. He was quite the handful, causing many disruptions throughout the day. On this particular afternoon, he had instigated yet another scuffle in the block center. I hurried over and explained the rules once again for sharing and the consequences for noncompliance. Almost immediately afterward, I heard the angry commotion again from his classmates.

I called on April. She was happily playing in the kitchen with her little girlfriends. They had a lovely tea party going on with play cupcakes and pastries arranged beautifully on the tablecloth.

"April," I said, "would you please go over and tell Manuel the rules for the block center. Tell him he has to share or he will lose his center time."

In hindsight, I should have taken more notice of her body language as she placed her teacup back on the saucer. I should have seen the reluctance as she laid her favorite doll back in its bed and tucked it in. She even patted it lovingly as if to assure her baby that she would be right back. Then I saw the smile leave her face as she replaced it with a business-as-usual expression and headed to face off with Manuel.

I had grown so dependent on April and so confident that she would handle every situation that I had actually gone on to helping another child. I was seated beside the other student, helping with a puzzle, when I felt the soft tap on my shoulder.

I turned to see April, standing with tears streaming down her face. "Mrs. Rodgers," she began, voice and lips quivering. "Manuel . . . he . . . he not listen to you in English, and he not listen to me in Spanish." It was as if the declaration somehow evidenced defeat on her part. Tears of frustration streamed down her precious cheeks.

Suddenly, the magnitude of the situation hit me with utter clarity. I had placed far too much stress on this little girl. Unintentionally, I was relying on her to help me run my classroom. She was my unpaid assistant, and I had just forced her to leave her baby in the kitchen unattended.

I pulled April to me, hugged her and wiped her tears. "Well, you just don't worry about Manuel," I said. "You go back and play. I will take care of Manuel."

She wiped the few remaining stray tears away and hurried back to her abandoned baby doll. In just a few minutes, I heard laughter and saw happy smiles in the kitchen.

My sweet, devoted little April. You were so mature, so helpful, and so eager to please that I forgot you were just a little girl. You taught me to never, ever again do that to you or any other child. The frustrations and responsibilities of my job were just that. My job. Not yours.

After all, I made you leave a baby unattended, and that was just all wrong.

Aaliyah

She was one you just wanted to take home with you. As cute as they come, she had a personality to match her perfect features—dark-brown hair in ringlet curls down her back, crystal-blue eyes. And the most innocent little voice with the slightest speech impediment. She could carry on a conversation on almost any subject, was a fashion diva, and kept up on the newest music trends. She was around adults more than other children, so Monday mornings were so interesting hearing her discuss all the events of the weekend. She adored her papa, and they were always on an adventure.

My assistant and I were constantly amused at Aaliyah's view of the adult world. It seemed to occupy much of her thoughts. At Christmas our Parent Teacher Organization opened a Santa's Workshop where children could do their shopping for their families and friends. The items were flashy, dime-store quality with a markup large enough to be a sizable fundraiser for the school. On the day before my class's scheduled shopping excursion, we got to browse and check off the gifts my students wished to purchase. We would then send the envelope home so the appropriate money could be sent in the following day.

I was watching Aaliyah browse the shelves and tables. She had quite the list going on. There were already several checkmarks, and she hadn't even reached the men's section, where I knew she would be selecting something for her beloved papa.

I was helping some of the other students with their browsing when I glanced over at Aaliyah standing in front of a waist-strap tool kit. I could just see the wheels turning. Her papa ran an auto repair shop. Of course the tools in this kit would not meet the quality-standard requirements of his business, but the thought would be lovely and show personal consideration by Aaliyah.

She asked the PTO worker for the price. By Aaliyah's reaction, I could tell she was dismayed at the reply.

I joined her at the table. "Aaliyah, how is your shopping going?" I asked, anticipating the usual "grownie" response.

"Okay, I guess." She sighed. "Dese toowel bwelts are expensive!"

She asked me to help her add up the cost of everything she had already listed. Not counting the tool belt, her items totaled $15.00. The tools would cost an additional ten.

"Oh no!" she lamented. "Dat's toooooo much. I tink I onlwee have ten dollars." She stood for a good minute staring into space. I could just see the wheels turning again. Then, with a "lightbulb just went on" look on her face, she approached the helper. "Do uuh take cwedit cards?"

A similar incident had happened with Aaliyah during rest time a few weeks earlier. I had been at the computer, looking over some educational toys to purchase for the classroom. Aaliyah had come to ask me a question and looked at the screen over my shoulder.

"Oh, I wike dose," she squealed quietly, pointing to a new kitchen-center set. "Do uuh wike dose?"

"Yes, I do, Aaliyah. They look fun!"

"Well, den qwick it," she said. "Dus muv de mouse, an qwick it!" She smiled. "It's eezy!"

But my favorite of all of Aaliyah's childhood views of the adult world came during rest time on another day.

She couldn't sleep and wanted a few minutes of rocking. I was all too happy to oblige. I pulled her up into my lap, and she snuggled down for her cherished one-on-one time. Suddenly, she sat up and patted my chest where her head had been. "When I get to be a teenager, I will have dose," she said, patting my unblessed chest.

"Oh you will?" I asked amused. "Is that when you get those? When you're a teenager?"

Yes, she nodded her head assuredly. "Dat's when you get 'em!"

"Oh," I said. "I see. Well, what about Mrs. Donovant?" I asked, looking over at a colleague who had just tiptoed in to leave a file on my desk.

"Yep! She's a teenager!" Aaliyah positively announced.

"Aaliyah, what about Miss Domica? Is she a teenager?" I asked, referring to my well-endowed assistant.

Aaliyah sat up and looked over at Miss Domica, who was placing the children's snacks on the table. Aaliyah's eyes grew wide and she drew in a long, exaggerated breath.

"Ohhh!" She said, nodding again. "She is WEALLY a teenager!"

Oh, my little Aaliyah. What a joy you were as I learned to look at the big, adult world through an innocent child's eyes. You simplified credit cards and teenagers. Two subjects that are often far too complicated.

Sadie

I always look forward to registration day. I get to meet all the candidates for the coming year's class. After they are signed in, I schedule their pre-school entrance test, and from these results I select my sixteen children. The program is designed to target the children who are in greater need of enrichment activities.

The light from Sadie's smile shone through the doorway before she and her grandfather entered. She was tall, slim, with blonde, shoulder-length hair and a grin that spread from ear to ear. She came straight to me and hugged my neck, then set about looking around the classroom. The grandfather was delightful. He was the caretaker while Sadie's mother worked, and he was a little distressed at losing his sidekick. I was still talking to him while my assistant looked through her paperwork. After only a few brief seconds, she passed the form back to me with Sadie's birth date circled in red. She was only three years old and wouldn't be four until months after the cut-off date.

"Mr. Creed," I began. "There's a problem. Sadie won't be eligible for pre-k until she's four."

Surprisingly, Sadie came running from across the room. She knew exactly what I had said and also knew what it meant. "You mean I can't come to school?" She began to cry before I could answer her.

Her grandfather tried to console her. "I'm sorry," he began. "I didn't know. She's real smart and wanted to come and—"

I interrupted him with a pat on his hand. "Mr. Creed, it's okay. It has nothing to do with her desire to come to school or how smart she is. I just can't test her until she's eligible, and that won't be until next year.

Sadie began to sob, tears flowing. Her grandfather looked at her helplessly. Trying to make her laugh, he tried a little diversion tactic. "What if I dance for you ladies? Will you let her in then?" He stood up and began flat-footing right there on the spot. I was so taken in by his attempt at bribery that I let him do a few more steps before I shook my head.

Sadie was still wailing. Then I had an idea. While her granddaddy and I had been talking, he had shared with me how much she loved dinosaurs and already knew all of the names. I went over to my shelves and selected a huge model of a T-Rex. I went to Sadie and took her gently away from her granddaddy.

"Here, Sadie," I said. "You take this dinosaur home with you and bring it back to me next year when you come back to be in my class."

She stopped crying and took the dinosaur, hugging it to her tightly.

Mr. Creed thanked me. Sadie nodded that she would take good care of the T-Rex, then waved, and they were out the door.

Fast forward to the following year. Sadie came back, was tested, and was happily accepted into my class. Little did I know then what a joy she would bring to my days—and for years to follow.

We were going over all the rules for the classroom and the school. I had all the children seated in a circle on the carpet. Sadie was seated beside little Gavin, (who also has a chapter in this book). He had scooted very close and had his arm around her. I allowed myself a second to smile at how sweet it was before I stepped in.

"Gavin, sweetie, take your arm off Sadie. She may not like that."

In a flash, she shot back. "Ohhh, I LIKE IT!"

And so began the year of laughs. Like the time I was teaching the class all about mammals. As I described that all mammals are covered with fur and feed milk to their young, Sadie raised her hand and shared that her mommy had fur but she shaved it off.

Or the time she excitedly told us that she was going to have a new baby sister and that she was going to look like a Carmella candy bar.

As much as I enjoyed Sadie in my classroom, the feeling was matched by the devotion she had for me. Not one single day passed that she didn't come straight to me from her granddaddy's car and give me a huge hug. She taught me that teachers do hold a special place in their students' hearts . . . if they want to be there.

Briella

I ended all my stories of children by sharing what I learned from them. This one is going to be a little different. I am going to start off by telling you what Briella taught me and also offering a word of advice. If you are going into teaching, be prepared. Be ready to laugh, to cry, to teach, to learn, to be patient, to be intuitive. And most of all, expect the unexpected—at all times. That's what Briella taught me.

She was a little Campbell Soup kid: round, plump features, golden blonde hair falling to her shoulders. By medical terms she was over the weight guidelines for her age, but the extent of just how much was well hidden under cute little floral tent dresses. She was from a home brimming with love and grandparents. Her mother and father were both professionals who worked outside the home. So her life to this point had been spent primarily with her great-grandparents. Occasionally, her grandparents would have her, but anyway, you get the picture. Grandparents usually mean spoiling, and Briella was happily in a soup pot of it.

She had virtually never been around children. Her vocabulary was that of a well-educated adult. As I was testing her for preschool, I asked her to count to ten for me. Briella asked if I wanted her to count in English or in Chinese. Certainly, the only reason Briella needed a year in pre-kindergarten was to socialize her with children her age. Academically she was ready for . . . maybe junior high?

I learned right away that Briella's tolerance level was very low. She had been used to having what she wanted when she first desired it. So patience was definitely a skill we would have to address. I was somewhat amused at the expression she kept on her face practically 100 percent of the time. It was an "everyone is getting on my last nerve" look. Adults, of course, call this "pissed off."

To continue my story of Briella, I must introduce another student, little Micah. (I will go into more detail in his own chapter.) Briefly, Micah had profound developmental issues: absolutely no language except for grunting and pointing, still drinking from a sippy cup, and no speed control. He was either motionless or running at top speed in any given direction. Quite a handful by himself, and I had fifteen others.

What every beginning teacher needs to be aware of—and they do not teach this in college—is that every school is required to have a fire drill during the first week of school. Now, that is well and good for first grade and beyond, but it is the pre-k and kindergarten teachers who must do the training for these mini field trips out of doors.

There are a host of factors that spell chaos for the pre-k teacher. First and foremost, fire evokes fear and, thus, the fight-or-flight response. You have to explain to the children that we are only "practicing" a life-or-death situation. The alarm itself scares the patootie out of them. So if you can survive that and get them in some type of line formation . . . Ooops! I forgot to mention that they don't know what a line is yet. You have to teach them that. Then you have to get them quietly out the door and past the all-too-inviting playground to stand stoically in said line formation, without saying a word, until another alarm rings to signal everyone back in. Do you get the picture?

So here we go. It's the second day of school, and suddenly, the fire drill alarm is sounded. My assistant and I exchange a look of horror and disbelief. We usually practice these in the room several times before the real thing—but the principal has sprung this one on us early.

I try to live by the philosophies "Never let them see you sweat" and "Keep calm and carry on." I immediately formulated an emergency plan and put it into action.

I took little Micah's hand and passed him off to my assistant. I instructed her to hold onto him and not let go. I would handle the rest. I managed to corral all the others, and using a choo-choo-train analogy, I had the remaining fifteen children following me, somewhat bewildered, out of the classroom. Of course, when we got outside and I had all the visual competition of playground, dozens of children, and the long-horned cows in the neighboring pasture, I had my work cut out for me. My assistant was having an equally difficult time keeping little Micah in tow. He was quick, and several times he wrenched his hand free and was off. She had to do some quick trotting and quick thinking to catch him before he got out of arm's length. The whole time, he was excitedly pointing and grunting and trying to comprehend this new adventure.

It's important to not only visualize what's happening with my little class but also school-wide. These are approximately 190 children, all involved in this practice drill, and they've all mastered the routine. They are in perfect lines and also perfectly quiet. Proudly, I'd had most of them in pre-k, and I taught them this. "You're Welcome, fellow teachers."

So, it's a beautiful day, the sun is shining, and the only movement on the hillside is little Micah running amok and my assistant trying to keep him still. All his classmates are standing in line, so exuberant that they have escaped the burning building unsinged.

Then, as I glanced proudly over my group, my eyes fell on Briella. She had one hand on her hip and had that annoyed look on her face as she watched Micah darting and grunting. I allowed myself one moment's amusement at her stance. Her little tent dress, her hip thrust out, and her expression were altogether too funny.

But funny was short lived. I suddenly saw her leave her place in line and go strutting up to where my assistant had just corralled Micah. With that one hand still on her hip, and her expression still registering disgust, she poked Micah with her other hand and asked, in a level loud enough to, I believe, echo throughout the hills, "What is f**king wrong with you?"

I don't know whose mouth dropped open the farthest, mine or my assistant's. I immediately tried to get to Briella, but I had forgotten my choo-choo train. As soon as I stepped out of line, the entire class tried to follow. So, I had to place each one back as I frantically tried to dash the twelve feet to Briella. I was too late. Because Micah had not responded to her first question, she repeated, much louder than before, "I said, 'WHAT IS F**KING WRONG WITH YOU?'"

At last I made it to her, amidst the gasps and stares of the entire school, grabbed her hand, and led her away from the group.

Still displaying that annoyed, "I can't believe I'm having to be here with these children" expression on her face, she looked up at me and matter-of-factly observed, "I guess I wasn't supposed to say that, was I?"

Always expect the unexpected . . . because it *will* happen!

Micah

I received a call from another pre-k teacher in the county on our first workday of the new school year. She told me of a child she had tested in her school zone who had failed every section of both tests. She had referred him to the preschool handicapped class, but for some reason, she had heard he was heading my way. She just wanted to give me a heads-up. He was out of my attendance zone, but he would be in my class. She suggested that I just keep accurate documentation and refer him once again for the handicapped class. She could not see him functioning in a regular classroom environment.

When I first met Micah and his mother, I was alarmed at his size. He was at least half the average size for a child his age. However, that was not the most alarming observation. Micah didn't speak. He grunted and pointed to communicate and have his needs met. But the other alarming piece to this puzzle was that his mother responded to those grunts and signals. During the meeting, I took mental notes of their interaction. Micah seemed to be curious and excited about his classroom, but it was his mother who would say, "Do you want this? Do you want that?" Or Micah would grunt and point and she would quickly give him what he wanted.

She appeared to be an older mother, probably in her early forties. I guessed that she had longed for a baby for years and had given up hope until this wonderful late-in-life surprise.

Micah was such an adorable little boy. He was very affectionate and seemed to be attached to his mommy. And it was quite apparent that he had her wrapped tightly around all his fingers, especially the pointy one.

He had dark-brown hair and tiny, pinprick freckles across his nose. He had pronounced facial expressions, possibly to aid his lack of vocabulary. It was easy to tell what Micah was thinking and feeling. He certainly had total command of every muscle in his little face. But what I saw as my biggest challenge would be awakening the muscles known as vocal chords.

I already knew what my plan of action was. While I fully understood this mom's heart—to take care of her son and keep him happy—it was this well-intended devotion that was somewhat crippling his development. Language is developed primarily out of the basic need to communicate our needs. If our needs are met without it, why bother? That had been Micah's discovery.

Thankfully, Micah loved school. Because I'm certain it was a rude awakening for him. I immediately let him know he would have to ask, or at least attempt to ask, for anything he wanted from me. At first it was very frustrating for him. He would point and grunt for a toy, and I would look at it then tell him what it was called. Often, I would take his hands gently in mine to prevent him from pointing. Then I would model the request. "May I have the truck?" Often, I would get only a semblance of the final word, but I would accept that to strengthen his attempt. What was so encouraging about this process was Micah's eagerness to please me. Soon, he was placing his own hands in mine to prevent himself from pointing. We graduated from one word to whole sentences in only a few months.

Now, during this time, language was not the only skill we were working on. At breakfast, on the first day of school, it was obvious that Micah had either been on a bottle or a sippy cup. His first attempt at drinking from a milk carton was a soaking disaster. So I poured the milk into a plastic cup, held Micah in my lap, and we proceeded from there. Within a week, he was getting more liquid in him than on him. He had also never fed himself. Using a spoon was new to him but not as difficult to learn as the cup.

Another obstacle my assistant and I faced in teaching Micah was the other children. We saw them doing the exact same thing his mother had done. Micah was just so adorable. All the children loved him and would go out of their way to take care of him. We had to train them to do pretty much what we did—force him to talk.

By Christmas Micah had made monumental progress. Even though his speech was monotone, resembling a robot's in lack of inflection, we could understand him. Things were so much simpler now. We knew if he understood directions because he could tell us. Classroom discipline had been easy with Micah because he had an agreeable temperament. But, as with all children, there came a day when he had to go to the time out chair due to a minor squabble during center time. We had to make sure he understood why he had to go. I will never forget the look on Micah's face as I sent him to the chair with the egg timer. I set it for five minutes. The memory of him in that little chair, shoulders drooped, head in hands, tears streaming down his face as he stared at the timer, will forever be in my mind. But he had to learn, just as we adults do, "That which doesn't kill us makes us stronger." My assistant and I had to share a tissue during those five minutes, which seemed to us much longer.

It was only a day or two after this that I had an early morning visitor in the office. I answered my page and found Micah's mom waiting for me in the lobby. There were tears in her eyes that momentarily frightened me, but the smile on her face softened my alarm. She had stopped by to tell me that the evening before, for the very first time in his four years of life, Micah had told her he loved her. He had actually said the words. She had tears and words of deepest, heartfelt appreciation. We exchanged hugs as I went back to my classroom.

Micah continued to flourish. By year's end, the only remnant of his pre-language days was the low grunting/humming noise he made to himself while he was either playing or working alone in centers. We occasionally tried to get him to stop, as it was irritating to some of the other children. But soon, they, and we, came to realize Micah didn't know he was doing it. He had accomplished so much in such a short amount of time that, if he found comfort in it, then we could all certainly overlook it.

Micah was a perfect example of how we can sometimes cripple without intention. In her effort to meet her son's needs, Micah's loving mother had prevented him from taking very fundamental steps in learning. She had to take a step back, as we did, and force him out of his comfort zone. That is true love. And it is the root of all learning.

Jack

Each school year, the classroom fills up with children, each carrying a different story. By this I mean they all have different families with developmental histories all their own. Some have had language-rich environments, while others have never held a storybook. A few have traveled and explored other parts of the state, country, and world. There may be just as many who have never journeyed out of the county.

The point is, we as teachers cannot ever assume that all our students have been exposed to the same set of rules, values, or learning experiences. We must get to know them first and go from there.

It was the very first day of school, and we had just finished several fun activities in the classroom. My reward to the children for following directions so well was to take them for their first visit to our playground.

It was a beautiful, sunny day. The temperatures were hitting near 80 degrees and the children scrambled to the playground like spring lambs let out to pasture.

Jack was one of the smallest children in the classroom. I had taught several from his family: brothers, cousins, and uncles. He was from hardworking, local, country stock used to being outdoors. He was just so cute. A good head shorter than his classmates, with blue eyes and a buzz-cut hairstyle. Also being one of the youngest, he still had that "baby look" about him.

He hit the playground wide open, so happy to be turned loose to play and explore.

I stood with my assistant, watching the frolicking and listening to their gleeful squeals. The warmth of the sun built in intensity on our backs. We could tell that by afternoon it would be a scorcher.

We were chatting about our plans for the upcoming week when I became aware of someone tapping my hip. I usually ignored such an intrusion because I always teach my students to never interrupt a conversation by pushing, poking, or tapping. If it's an emergency—and I specify fire, flood, blood, or vomit—they are to vocally say, "Excuse me," and then state the emergency at hand. But this being the first day of school, I hadn't gone over all the rules yet. So I finished my sentence and then looked down at the area of tapping.

It took me a few confused seconds to register what I was seeing. I recognized that it was Jack, because it was Jack's little head, but it was sitting atop a body that looked unfamiliar to me. It was as if I could not comprehend his appearance. Then, like a jolt, I realized why he looked strange. He didn't have a stitch of clothes on except his little "tighty whities." He had removed all of his clothes and was pushing the pile at me as if he wanted me to hold them.

"Jack," I said forcefully. "You cannot take your clothes off on the playground. Put them back on immediately!"

"But I'm hot," he protested. Suddenly, this school playground didn't hold as much appeal as it had a few moments ago. Obviously, Jack had been used to playing in his skivvies.

A week hadn't passed when I discovered another activity Jack had been accustomed to performing in the great outdoors. We were once again on our playground. One of my little girls came dashing to me shouting, "Excuse me. Look at Jack!"

It wasn't fire, blood, or vomit, but it was an emergency. Jack was standing at the corner of the playground, his back to me. From the position of his pants around his ankles, I knew what was going on in front. "Jack," I called.

He completed his emergency, pulled up his pants, and came to me.

"Jack, you do not pee-pee on the playground! You must go inside and use the bathroom." Once again, the look on his face signaled that he thought I had some really strange rules.

It was a good thing Jack was so cute because he certainly was a handful. He loved seeing just how much he could get into. I wasn't really worried. I knew I could tame him.

One day, he thought he would make all his classmates laugh by pulling his shirt up over his head. He got stuck and I let him sweat it out for a while. He squirmed and grunted, and finally, the tears came as he got hopelessly tangled up in his own sleeves. I had to fight the urge to help him, knowing he needed this little scare. I was right. After I thought he had learned his lesson, I set him free. He never tried that again.

But with all his mischievousness and propensity to do the wrong things, Jack had a side that wanted to do the right thing. He was a true gentleman at heart, even though he was a little rough around the edges.

Each Thanksgiving, I teach a unit on table manners and dining etiquette. The little boys learn how to escort and seat the little girls at the table and also how to help them up and escort them away. They learn table manners, how to set a proper table, and rules concerning napkins and silverware usage. On the day before school lets out for the Thanksgiving holiday, we have a meal served in our classroom. All the children dress in their Sunday best, and I set a table with my best linens, china, and crystal. The couples who have practiced together have a lovely meal showing off all they have learned.

Before we ever begin practicing, my assistant and I pair the children off in couples. We try to make sure they are compatible so the whole experience will be enjoyable. When it came to Jack, we knew who he wanted to be with. He absolutely adored Blaire. He would follow her at recess. He wanted to play with her at center time. He wanted to sit with her at breakfast and lunch. Yes, he was smitten with the love bug. So we knew we would have no objections from Jack if we told him that he was going to escort Blaire.

However, we knew Blaire might not share his enthusiasm. She was well over a foot taller than Jack and outweighed him by at least thirty pounds. Even at four and five years of age, some girls are sensitive to this. Thankfully, Blaire was agreeable to the pairing, and we began to practice.

The first thing I like to teach them is escorting, simply because it is so adorable to watch. After we are comfortable with that, we move to seating. Several couples had already successfully practiced with the boy pulling the chair out, seating the young lady, and pushing the chair under the table.

Then it was Jack and Blaire's turn. I couldn't help smiling as I saw how proud he was to be walking with Blaire on his arm. He led her to the table and pulled the chair out. Blaire sat down obligingly and waited. Jack stepped behind her chair to push her under the table.

He gave the chair a firm push. Nothing happened. Blaire was still in the same place, a good foot from where she was supposed to be. Jack pushed again, straining so hard that a little grunt escaped him. Still nothing. Blaire still sat. Not to be outdone and let his woman down, little Jack stretched his body out horizontally to the ground and pushed with all his might. His jaw was rigid with the effort, cheeks flushed a fiery red and a long groan emanated from within. Blaire was like a mountain that could not be moved. I stepped in and whispered into Blaire's ear, urging her to help Jack out and give herself a little scoot.

She obliged, and with his next thrust, Blaire was successfully under the table. Wiping sweat from his moist brow, Jack took his seat beside his beloved, exhausted.

Oh, my little Jack. You taught me that even those who are a little rough around the edges can have hearts in the right place. It was worth learning a little polish when it was for someone you loved.

Jason

I suppose I should have seen the signs. They were there right from the beginning. When my assistant and I went for our scheduled home visit, Jason took me to see the red Toyota he was working on. He said he was going to take me to West Virginia in it. Then, when we toured his home, he wanted me to climb up on his bunk bed to see if I was afraid. He even asked me to see his treehouse, just to make sure I was not fearful of heights and that I could climb all the way up in it.

But truthfully, I had no idea, no inkling that Jason was in love with me and wanted me to marry him.

Jason and his brother Lucas came to me as a matched set. Fraternal twins, they were as different as night and day, salt and pepper, up and down—well, you get the picture. Jason was slightly thinner, more talkative, and didn't mind domestic jobs. Lucas was muscular, serious, attentive to academics, and loved sports. He didn't want to be caught in the kitchen. Both boys were equally endearing. Lucas usually headed to the block section during center time. All the little girls loved that Jason would play house with them at centers. He would dress their dolls for them, wear an apron, and wash the dishes. What woman wouldn't love him?

Just about the only traditionally masculine interest he had was working on cars. His father had given him an old, junked Toyota that Jason would tinker with. He had high hopes of getting it on the road, with me in it, and heading for West Virginia.

I had noticed that Jason was always asking if he could help me around the classroom. And he asked me if I was married or had a boyfriend. All these are questions children ask all the time, and I didn't give it a second thought . . . until that home visit.

Some pre-k teachers do their required home visits before school starts. I always like to schedule mine for September. By then the children know my assistant and me and are thrilled to have us come to their homes. Before that, they are generally afraid and hide.

Jason and Lucas's mother greeted us warmly. She was a bus driver for our school, so I knew her well. After we had made the rounds and seen everything they wanted us to see, we went to the kitchen. Jennifer had made us coffee cake and tea.

As we were settling in to enjoy our refreshments, Jen dropped the bomb on me. She said, "Betsy, I love you but I want my ring back."

I know from my expression that she knew I needed more of this story than what she had given.

She began. It seems that Jason had been talking to the

little girls at school, and he told them that he loved me and wanted to marry me. They told him that he would have to give me a ring. So that evening, when she took her ring off to wash the dishes, Jason had taken it and put it in his pocket to give to me.

"But, Jen!" I gasped. "He never gave me a ring."

"Oh, I know that," she said. "He confessed that he lost it before he could give it to you. I just want you to please be on the lookout for it. He doesn't know where he lost it."

I was heartsick for her. She said she had vacuumed the house twice and checked the bag. She had searched all his pockets. At this point, she felt it was gone for good.

Home visits are designed to connect school to the home. Children are more comfortable in a learning environment where they know a connection is made with their parents, siblings, and with their teacher, so right at this moment, I knew what to do.

Growing up, I had a friend who was Catholic. I was raised a Baptist but often went to Mass with him. One day, he was having lunch at my house with my mother and me. She had been working in the yard that morning but had come in to enjoy lunch with us. Suddenly, she looked down at her hand and screamed. The diamond was missing from the setting in her ring. She covered her face and went running to the bedroom. I could see her crying—and my mother *never* cried. My father had passed away when I was only eight years old. The engagement ring had unmeasurable sentimental value.

Knowing she had been working in the yard all morning, it seemed a hopeless situation. However, my friend didn't think so. He immediately dropped to his knees, and I will forever remember his prayer.

"Saint Anthony, Saint Anthony, please look around. Something dear is lost that must be found."

At *precisely* that moment, we saw a flash of light near the window. The sun was reflecting on something resting on the quarter-round. I followed the light that led me right to my mother's diamond, balanced precariously on the quarter-inch molding.

I was shocked beyond words. My friend, however, was not. "It never fails," he said. He explained how St. Anthony, in the Catholic faith, is the patron saint of the lost.

In the years since that miracle in our kitchen, the prayer had worked countless times, without fail, for myself and all my family. So now it was time to pass it along. "Jen, I said, "I will find your ring. I am going to say St. Anthony's prayer."

She listened while I recited the prayer, which by now had become an integral part of my life. Her smile was a mix of hope and disbelief.

My assistant and I left the house and headed back to school. Theirs had been the last home visit for the day. Within a half hour, I got the excited call. It was Jen. She had found the ring in the middle of her bedroom carpet after we left. It was lying there, in full view, on a carpet that had been vacuumed twice.

Now it was Jennifer who was shocked, and it was me who was not.

Oh, my little fiancé, Jason. You taught me much more than that little boys sometimes fall in love with their teachers. You taught me that we are all in this together. The connection between home and school and parents and teachers runs deep. You gave me the opportunity to share faith and pass along a miracle, just as all parents share their miracles with me each day. After all, children are the greatest miracle of all.

Hanna

Hanna's cards were stacked against her from the very beginning. We can only do so much to help a child when everything we do at school gets undone when they go home. And speaking of a house of cards, she had a "full house," which is good in a game but not in Hanna's world.

First, there was a live-in grandmother with mental issues. She saw people who weren't really there. Not only did she see them, but they also engaged in conversation that would often result in her becoming combative.

There was also the young, unemployed mother. For some reason she either couldn't hold down a job or she never bothered to look for one. There was no means of transportation, so if she couldn't get there on foot, she didn't go. So if Hanna got sick during the day, Mom would have to walk miles to get her, which also meant that Hanna would have to walk home. Often, I would get permission to drive them. Then there was Hanna's brother. Very sneaky but, overall, a good student. No demon, but not an angel either.

Yet Mom held Brother up to Hanna all the time. "Look how good your brother is. Why can't you be like your brother?" Sometimes, I thought Brother set Hanna up just to see her get punished.

So Hanna came to see me with a history that made her prone to mood swings, outbursts of anger, and feelings of alienation. She was an adorable little girl. If engaged in a conversation, she would delight you with her imagination and rich language. She adored picture books. I learned early on that if Hanna was having a difficult time settling down, a stack of storybooks beside her worked miracles. She would sit and take each book, turn every page carefully, and a magical world would verbally come spilling out. At home, when she was talkative, or active, or anything that required attention from anyone, she was required to sit on her bed for the entire evening with nothing to do. I began sending books home with her so she would have them to keep her company when she was on that bed.

Again, I could not control how Hanna was treated at home, but I was certainly able to set the stage at school. Hanna learned that she was safe, respected, and loved. She was disciplined with consistency and fairness. And like a little flower that is tended correctly, she flourished and blossomed.

She longed to be able to read the books she loved to look at, so learning the sounds of the letters was easier than learning the letter names. Hanna was a kinesthetic learner so I always made certain she had hands-on activities.

She was so inquisitive and didn't hesitate to ask questions about anything new or puzzling. As we were crammed in our little bathroom one day during our first tornado drill, Hanna broke the awkward silence by inquiring, "Can the tomato find us in here?"

Hanna had so much "bottled energy." Knowing that Hanna spent a great deal of time each evening confined to her room, I knew she needed a physical release. Each morning, I found that starting the day with running the track near our playground helped her tremendously. That physical release would help her corral that energy, as needed, in the classroom.

Hanna carried so much emotional baggage around with her, too much for her young mind to comprehend or find words for.

One morning, she arrived at school withdrawn and sullen. She entered the classroom and immediately headed to our little library that was furnished with soft beanbag chairs and stuffed animals. Several attempts by other children to talk to her or engage her in play with them had resulted in angry rejections.

I saw tears welling up in her eyes, so I went to her. I pulled her up into my lap as she clutched one of the stuffed bears tightly to her chest. "What's wrong, Hanna?" I asked. "Can you tell me what's happened?"

I could feel her shaking her head as she clutched the bear even tighter.

I tried again. "I might be able to help you if you can tell me what's wrong."

She was motionless for a few seconds, and then she pulled back and looked at me with eyes dampened by tears and sadness. "Look inside my words," she pleaded. "Listen to what I'm thinking."

When I said goodbye to Hanna at year's end, I didn't know what her future held. I gathered up all my extra work pages, some storybooks, and outdated manipulatives and took them by Hanna's home. She ran out to my car to meet me and threw her little arms around my neck. She was so full of love and smiles. But it was her extra energy that I feared would present a problem. I hoped that everyone in her future would look for creative ways to channel that energy instead of sedating it. She was a hard one to let go.

My little Hanna. I know there's a saying, "If you love something, let it go." But you're one I feared to let go. I was afraid that I was going to be the last to hear those fantastic imaginative stories that she released from the books she loved.

I learned from Hanna that I have ever so much to learn in keeping children safe from their environments and from conflicting methods of education. I learned that I have to do the very best I can, and then I have to let them go.

Jonah

Jonah was adorable. Big blue eyes that popped above a freckled face framed by white, cornsilk hair. As his mother and father registered him for my class, they kept shaking their heads and reaching over sympathetically to pat my hand. Throughout the registration process, I occasionally glanced at Jonah exploring his new surroundings. Eyes wide with excitement and anticipation, he darted around, touching everything and letting out a squeal of joy when he found my block area. I smiled at this but noticed his parents exchange a worried glance and then reach over and pat my arm once again.

As they exited the room, pulling a whimpering Jonah with them, who was pleading to stay with me, I went to the block area to clean up and prepare the room for the first day of school. I paused in amazement at the block city Jonah had quickly built on the carpet. I reluctantly took the buildings apart, putting the blocks back in their big bin.

The beginning of every school year is always such an exciting time. All the little personalities come together, new friendships start forming, and I begin the process of discovering what makes each child "tick." Being a relatively new teacher, I was still trying to find that gray area. The area that administration says I must do—and the area I feel comfortable doing.

I do not mind constructive noise, the excited conversation and laughter of children at play. However, my tolerance level did not always match that of my superiors. This particular principal liked quiet . . . and lots of it.

Jonah was a noise machine. He talked excitedly to his friends from the moment he arrived until his three o'clock departure. As soon as he entered through the door, he started working the room, making sure no one was left out. I found his enthusiasm delightful but knew my principal would mark me down on classroom management if he ever walked in and heard Jonah's running commentary.

So this dilemma began to concern me, and I found myself feeling a mounting level of exasperation at Jonah as he disrupted every lesson with his comments, his questions, and his comical antics which delighted his classmates. I then recalled his parents patting my arm and knew this was their way of telling me, "We know what you're going to face."

I loved Jonah. I adored his spirit, and I felt so bad about myself as I finally resorted to the practice of "time out" when he interrupted the class with his commentaries. Even in time out, Jonah would find a way to talk, regardless that no one was listening, and the little guy even found a way to stand on his head in the time out chair!

Then I noticed Jonah changing. As his trips to time out increased so did his negative behavior. My frustration at trying to keep the class at an acceptable noise level for the administration's approval was resulting in mounting frustration in Jonah and in me.

Finally, one day, as I found myself pointing Jonah to the time out chair yet again, I looked straight into those blue eyes, and I saw the same frustrated look that I was feeling. But I also saw something more. I saw hurt, and possibly a tear, although I had never seen Jonah cry. I knelt down and pulled him close. He wrapped his arms around me, and the dam broke on those tears. He sobbed.

I finally found my voice. "Jonah, I'm so sorry to have to send you to the time out chair. But I have to. Why do you talk so much?"

After a few seconds, he pulled away from me and looked straight into my eyes this time. "Because," he began as he wiped tears away from those baby blues. "I have so much to say."

So there I had it. And it was the undeniable truth. Jonah did have a lot to say, and it was, in fact, interesting and delightful, and I should be ashamed for hushing his spirit.

That night, I devised my plan, and the very next morning, I put it into action. Every morning, for fifteen minutes, we had Jonah time. He had the floor and could tell all the interesting things in his world. He called up friends who also wanted to say something, and I even incorporated some instruction by teaching the children the proper way to introduce one to another. Jonah was like a little news reporter, and he looked forward to sharing. It became one of my favorite times of day, as it was Jonah's. And he knew that he would lose this time if he disrupted instruction, so gradually, the problem subsided.

Sweet, sweet, Jonah, I will forever miss him. He taught me that children *do* have so much to say, and we, as adults, *need* to listen.

Gavin

She just hadn't had a girl yet, but she was going to try one more time. I'm referring to Gavin's mom. At present she had two little redheaded boys, and I had the delight of teaching both of them. Little country boys, three years apart, with deep Southern drawls and sweetness beyond words. Bless-your-heart sweetness sporting hair that was the color of pumpkins in the autumn fields.

Both boys were precious in the classroom. High energy that needed corralling but so eager to please me that it wasn't difficult. They didn't have a bounty of toys or books at home, so they bounded into the classroom each day ready to read and play with everything. I recall that they both adored craft time and loved to paint. And no matter how much I wanted to hang their works in the classroom, they each showed so much disappointment at the thought of leaving their creations that I had usually allowed their paintings to go home to Mama. They were a close family—a lot of love there.

As the due date for Gavin's newest sibling approached, I noticed an uneasiness about Gavin throughout the day. He wanted to paint more pictures for his mama, he had a few unexplained tummy aches, and he came to me for more hugs than usual. These are behaviors often seen after the arrival of a new baby but usually not before.

Then came the morning that Gavin didn't come to school. I was hopeful that this was the day he would get his new little sister. We had already been through our morning circle time and had made our way into the cafeteria for breakfast. I was finishing opening up cereals and milks when in walked Gavin—no smile beaming from his face. He threw his book bag over into the corner and headed toward the breakfast line without even speaking.

"Gavin," I asked. "Why are you late?"

"My mama is having the baby," he said in a weary tone, shoulders drooping noticeably.

"Oh, Gavin," I squealed. "Aren't you just so excited?"

"I don't know, Mrs. Rodgers. She has to push real hard on her Lucy 'til the baby comes out!"

Oh well . . . I did ask!

And I laughed all the way to the hospital that afternoon as I went to see Gavin's mama and his new baby brother, who was born sporting the same carrot top as the other two boys. After sharing the story with his mama, I told her that I was relieved that the baby *was* a boy, because if it had been a girl, I would always have thought of her as "Lucy."

Sweet little worried Gavin. He taught me that children worry greatly about many events that we, as adults, view as joyous. We need to be careful that they don't have more information than their little brains can process.

After all, pushing on one's "Lucy" hurts *really* bad!

Rosa

Rosa had bright, chinquapin eyes and tightly corn-rowed hair tied with colorful ribbons that always matched her starched dresses. I looked forward to her giggles and bubbly personality. Although she did seem to have a few fast friends, she definitely was adored by all her classmates.

I noticed right away that Rosa was a walking inventory of her surroundings. She was the one who noticed when I changed the bulletin boards and immediately knew who was absent. If I moved seats around, she voiced, quite to my dismay, who no longer had the "special" chair. The chair was special simply because it was the only blue one. I learned that year with Rosa to always have all the chairs alike.

One morning, I clip-clopped into the classroom with my briefcase in hand and looking, in my opinion, quite professional in my red pencil skirt, camel pumps, and white-collared sweater. As I busied myself getting all the materials out for the day, I noticed Rosa's sharp eyes following me as I moved about the room. As I glanced her way, I would offer an occasional smile, expecting one in return. She did not. Yet her interest in me, as well as her stare, continued.

Finally, as I was writing the date on the blackboard, she spoke. "Mrs. Rodgers, when you got dressed this morning, did you think those shoes went with what you're wearing?"

Shocked and surprisingly embarrassed, I answered, "Why, yes, Rosa, I did. Do you think I made a bad choice?"

"Yes, ma'am," she quickly retorted with a slight look of disgust crossing her face. "You should have worn your red ones."

Oh, my little Rosa, my fashion diva. She taught me that little eyes are always watching, always taking in every detail. They may often see what you want them to see . . . but *always* what you don't.

Dalton

I'm a country gal, so naturally, I am drawn to little, country, farm-raised children. Those are the kids who learn to cook by age five, can do their own laundry, make their beds, and do all sorts of useful things before they grow up and leave home.

Dalton was a splendid example of such a child. He lived so far back in the sticks that when my assistant and I went to his home for our pre-school home visit, I had to park my four-wheel drive and we walked the rest of the way to his house. It was actually a trailer perched precariously on the side of a mountain. There was no phone or TV in the home, but we could hear music, laughter, and foot stomping as we approached the front door.

As we knocked, everything went still, and the door was suddenly flung open. There was Dalton, cheeks flushed, smiling from ear to ear. His parents started off our conference by telling us they had been dancing. Since they didn't have a TV, internet access, or a PlayStation, their entertainment was reading, playing cards, listening to the radio, and dancing. Dalton loved to dance. As we talked, I glanced around the room at all the drawings and family photos taped to the wall. These were happy people who enjoyed their child and each other.

Not long after this visit, we were having some music in our classroom. Dalton, as usual, was leading the class in some rather unique, high-stepping dance steps that reminded me of Gomer Pyle on the old Andy Griffith series. All the little girls in the class just adored Dalton. Being quite the dancer had earned him a "following."

After music, we divided up for centers, and I suddenly saw Dalton running top speed around the room with Laura and Abby in hot pursuit. I stopped the chase by grabbing Dalton, who seemed grateful for the intervention.

"What's going on here?" I asked.

Wiping sweat from his brow, he gasped. "They're trying to kiss me."

"Oh, is that so," I replied. "Well, I'll take care of this."

Leaving Dalton and trying to hide a smile that threatened to give away my amusement, I walked to the girls. After they confessed that they were indeed trying to kiss him, I sent them to the time out chairs for a little reflection time.

Then I went back to Dalton. He was still wiping the sweat off his face. "Dalton," I said. "You must not run in the classroom even if someone is after you. Just come and tell me. Okay?"

"Okay," he said.

I should have stopped there, but I didn't. Pulling him close so I could see that sweet little country-boy face, I asked, "Dalton, tell me, why are all the little girls trying to kiss you?"

"I don't know, Mrs. Rodgers," he said. "I have my pants on!"

Oops!

I was still laughing to myself that afternoon as I stopped to do grocery shopping at the local market. As I was selecting some produce, I heard a familiar laugh. Turning around, I saw Dalton in a shopping cart being pushed by his mother. Smiling at my good fortune of running into them, I approached and whispered the day's events into her ear.

She turned beet red and burst out laughing. Seems the expression "I have my pants on" is actually something her husband says when he doesn't have time for any fun. Except when Dalton had said it, an important word was left out. Her husband says, "I have my *work* pants on," meaning he's ready for work so there's no time for anything until he gets back home.

Oh, Dalton, my little, mountain-dancing country boy. You taught me to always think before I ask one question too many.

Hank

The woman who sat in front of me on registration day had deep-set wrinkles etching a road map of years or worry across her face. Her hair was thinning, seemingly more from malnutrition than age. Her voice was so soft that her words were barely audible. The smile she offered, however, was warm and genuine. The boys with her were dashing about the room, roughhousing and pulling toy after toy from the shelf.

Before I step in and control a situation like this, I like to give the parent the chance. She sat still and solemn, seemingly oblivious to the chaos around her. I stood and called the boys to a table where I had colorful wooden puzzles laid out enticing them to play. In seconds they were engaged and playing contentedly.

I turned back to the woman still seated at the table, and she began to tell her story. Her son had been left with the two boys when his wife went off to sow her wild oats or to help someone else sow theirs. So she had stepped in to help him out, and then, unexpectedly, he had oats that needed sowing as well. So now this grandmother had both boys.

"I do the best I can," she offered. "But they're just real active boys."

I discovered that I would only be getting Hank that year. The other would follow the year after. After doing all the necessary paperwork, and hearing a few more details of this weary grandmother's life story, it was time for me to meet my new student.

"Hank," I called. "Would you come here and talk to me a little bit?"

He immediately got up and, still holding a piece, reluctantly left his puzzle. Then he took the few steps back and snapped it into place. I noticed that he had worked all the puzzles correctly. He then slowly, and quite shyly, approached me.

He had deep, dark-chocolate eyes, brown tousled hair, and perfect features. He looked like a kid you'd see walking barefoot down a dirt road with a fishing pole in his hand. As he looked at me, I noticed that he kept his head either turned slightly downward or to the side so that his eyes never met me straight on but always with a sideways glance. Yet he didn't divert his eyes. They locked onto mine and stayed there.

"Hank, are you looking forward to coming to school?"

He nodded slightly. No smile or change in his expression, just a nod.

His grandmother spoke for him. "He doesn't talk very much, but he's real bright . . . and he's real active," she warned again.

So began my year with Hank. I found out very quickly that Hank was indeed active. But there was also a level of "scrappiness" about him that made him slightly aggressive with his classmates. Right away, I had reports of "Hank slapped me," or "Hank took my block. "He pushed me." "Hank knocked over my tower!" Since all this was happening during the first week of school, I wasn't too worried. Pre-k teaching is definitely not for wimps. You are responsible for corralling all those "me first" attitudes and behaviors that come together for the first time.

Soon it was the second week of school and the time that I preferred to schedule the home visits required in the pre-k program. The half-hour visit in each child's home helps us get to know the children better.

The premise for the visits is that it strengthens the home and school connection, making the child feel more comfortable. We always emphasize that it is not a home inspection, and we only go where the parent or guardian allows. So this varies drastically from home to home. Some give us the grand tour, and I have found myself climbing up into tree houses and bunk beds, and sitting down to homemade refreshments, all the way to just sitting on the front porch.

When we arrived at Hank's house, I was slightly uneasy about the condition of the yard. It was so littered with debris, junked cars, abandoned mowers, and broken toys that we had to step carefully to get to the front door. From past experience I know that if someone is this unconcerned about the curb appeal of their home, inside can only be worse.

Again, I emphasize, these are not home inspections. I merely observe my surroundings as anyone does when they go anywhere. Yet these observations help me to better understand the children I have coming to me every day.

The door opened on the first knock. Hank was standing there, same dark eyes, same solemn face, but right away I was alarmed. He was wearing a pull-up and nothing else. He turned slightly and yelled, "Mama, Teacher's here."

I was momentarily confused until I saw the grand-mother appear at the door. It was only at that moment that I became aware that Hank called her "Mama."

She smiled that same warm smile and invited us in. My assistant and I exchanged one brief glance at each other as if to confirm, "I've got your back and you've got mine."

We stepped inside.

It's always a surprise what stirs emotion in me to the point of drawing tears. Sometimes, it's a movie, often it's an old song. Cards and letters from my children always do it. And today, seeing where little Hank lived, did it. I had to brush the evidence away quickly before it streamed down my cheeks. I immediately wished we were back in the yard. The room we were in, I think, was supposed to be the living room or den. All the furniture was buried beneath dirty clothes and trash. She had three wooden chairs placed in the center of the floor for us to sit on.

I had briefly entertained the thought that our scheduled visit had been forgotten . . . but these chairs proved otherwise.

As we discussed Hank's first two weeks of school, I observed him and his brother running in and out of the room, each holding a half-eaten corn dog. Both were wearing pull-ups, and it was well past lunchtime. With Hank being four, and his brother being three, I guessed they still wore the pull-ups to bed at night. So the thought that they still had on the night's damp pants made me so sad.

I turned my attention back to Hank's grandmother, with her weary face and warm smile. I remembered what she had said to us two weeks before. *She was doing the best she could.* I thought of how hard this must be for her, raising two very young, very active boys with no income and no help from her son or daughter-in-law. The house, the yard, and her face—all reflected her depression.

We discussed Hank's behavior at school, and I related how I would not tolerate aggressiveness, and I would be correcting that. I asked her what she did when the boys fought, and basically, the response I got was that she just looked away. It was all too much for her. As we talked I was aware that Hank kept peeking around the door at us. I called him over and we talked briefly, but his shyness soon won and he retreated once again behind the door. My assistant and I left shortly afterward, both of us carrying an emotional load that we hadn't had thirty minutes before.

Back at school on Monday, I began a strict discipline plan to correct Hank's aggressive behavior. I was consistent. If he violated anyone's personal space or was aggressive in any way, he lost precious center time, which he loved. He always obeyed and took his timeouts without any defiance. I looked for any opportunity, even if it was just five minutes without an altercation, to praise Hank for good behavior. Whenever I rewarded him, or hugged him, his expression never changed. He "allowed" me to hug him, but he never hugged back.

Always, in the back of my mind, was the image of Hank's home. I only saw the one room, but I could imagine the rest. As I tucked Hank in for naptime that day, I noticed that he didn't have a stuffed animal to snuggle. I went to my closet and retrieved a big soft bear from my Goodwill stash. As I tucked it under Hank's arm, he sat up and stared at it for a moment. Then I watched as he covered it up and lay down beside it. He didn't hold it close like other children do their stuffed animals. He just lay beside it.

As the weeks went by, Hank's behavior began to improve. He had fewer trips to time out and even began to develop some solid friendships. His grandmother was right. He was very bright and quickly displayed mastery of all the pre-k skills. His report card reflected solid progress.

Christmas vacation was approaching, and I nominated Hank and his family for our Angel Tree, and then quickly pulled his name as my angel. I knew what he needed.

The morning of our class Christmas party, as I made my rounds during center time, I pulled Hank close and asked, "Hank, are you excited about Christmas coming?"

His answer will never be forgotten. "I don't want Christmas to come," was his soft-spoken reply.

It took me so off guard that I asked him to repeat.

"I don't want Christmas to come," he said again.

I had never heard a four-year old say that. Ever.

"What do you mean, Hank? Why?"

"Mama says I can't come to school at Christmas." He looked at me with that familiar sideways glance that I had come to love.

Chalk that response up as another tearjerker in me, as it certainly started the flow. I had to find a tissue quickly. Here I had a four-year-old boy who would rather come to school than have Christmas come. Possibly because, here at school, he had food, he had mental stimulation, he was warm, and he had love shown to him all the time in the form of strict discipline followed by warm hugs.

I thought of Hank constantly over the two weeks' vacation. I wondered if he was warm. I wondered if he was in wet pull-ups. I wondered if he was enjoying all the gifts I had left for him and his family. And I also hoped that his grandmother, in the midst of her weariness and her depression, would find a light to help her carry on.

Spring came, and Hank continued to thrive at school. His behavior had improved remarkably. He participated in group readings, and math and science emerged as his subjects of choice. He was indeed bright. Very bright!

One day near Spring Break, I recall Hank being very withdrawn all morning. His little face was sullen, and he sat alone in the library rather than join his friends in centers. I asked him if he wanted to lie down and he replied he did.

I got out his mat, blanket, and stuffed bear and put him over in the corner of the room. As I watched him getting comfortable, I noticed him do something that made the breath catch in my throat. He picked up his bear, looked at it for a moment, then squeezed it tightly to his chest and pulled the cover to his chin.

I walked over to Hank and knelt beside him. Those chocolate-brown eyes looked straight into mine. "Hank, are you okay? Does your tummy hurt?"

He closed his eyes as if that would help him concentrate on all his internal organs. He slowly opened his eyes and, in a whispered, almost inaudible voice, answered, "I don't think it's my tummy. I think it's my heart."

I made the decision then and there to make a phone call to his grandmother to find out if anything different was going on at home. I discovered that Daddy had shown up briefly the night before, made an appearance, stirred up the boys enough to satisfy his surface-level paternal notions, and left them before breakfast. He still had those oats . . .

I walked back to my classroom, feeling my heart aching probably the same way Hank's was. I opened the door, went straight to Hank, knelt beside him, and pulled him up to me without saying a word. And for only a few short seconds, for the very first time, Hank hugged back.

Oh, my little Hank. You taught me that teachers have a much greater responsibility than teaching S.O.L.s and academic skills. Sometimes, we are the only bandaid for a broken heart.

Julie

It was Friday, the end of a typical pre-k week. Things had run smoothly, and I can't recall anything out of the ordinary happening, which is very unusual. We had completed an interesting unit on protecting our environment, and the children had learned how to reduce, reuse, and recycle. We had made posters about all the ways we can save our natural resources, and for four-year-olds, I was impressed by all their ideas.

We were at breakfast and all sixteen children were seated, contentedly eating their cereal, toast, or eggs. My assistant was seated at one end of the long table and I at the other. In this way, we were both available to easily monitor the class. The children usually requested help from the nearest adult.

But this morning, Julie was actually seated closer to my assistant's end of the table. Julie was such a wholesome-looking little girl. She had sweet little curls, plump, rosy cheeks, and resembled, quite frankly, the little Campbell's Soup kids. She was quite an animated child, using her eyes and dramatic voice inflections to get her stories across.

I had noticed that she wasn't her usual chatterbox self this morning and was gazing ahead as she ate her toast as if some far-off scene had her attention. Suddenly, she jumped up from the table and came running to me. For her to bypass my assistant's close proximity and come dashing the length of table to me let me know this was going to be a serious issue.

"Mrs. Rodgers," she practically yelled, "I HAVE to tell you something!" Her eyes were wide, and she seemed to be extremely upset with what was on her mind. She had grabbed my attention, as well as everyone else's.

"What is it, sweetness?" I asked. Always having a pet name for the kids is my trademark.

"It's just awful! I can't tell you about it, but I *have* to!"

I had already learned that "awful" can have a host of meanings, from puppies getting killed in the road to having to eat Brussel sprouts for dinner. So I braced myself. "Go ahead and tell me if it's bothering you," I encouraged her.

"Okay." She took a deep breath and began her awful story. "This morning, while Daddy was in the shower . . . well . . . Mama . . . she, well . . . she got in the shower with him without her clothes on. I saw her get in the shower with Daddy!"

I just hated having to hold back my smile at this one, but I simply had to. Julie needed someone to sympathize with her awful confusion. "Oh, Julie," I said, pulling her close. "Do you know what your mommy and daddy were doing taking a shower together like that?"

She shook her head violently; partly, I think, to answer no, but also to shake off the visual image from her little head.

"Julie, do you remember this week that we've been learning ways to conserve our natural resources?"

She nodded. "Yes."

"Well, your mommy and daddy were conserving water, that's all. You must have gone home and told them all you had been learning, and they decided they were also going to find ways to reduce, recycle, and reuse."

"Oh!" Julie beamed, and a smile broke across her face. She returned to her seat, happily chatting again and eating the rest of her breakfast.

My assistant was hiding her face to prevent the children from seeing her unharnessed laughter. She finally came to me. "Mrs. Rodgers, boy, am I glad she came to you with that one! How did you keep a straight face?"

"What do you mean, how did I keep a straight face?" I asked her. "I'm quite upset about it." I added, forcing my expression to reflect my words.

"What? What do you mean, upset?" she asked me.

"Well, I'm upset because it's quite obvious that my kids' parents lead more interesting lives than me!"

Then we both laughed.

Ah, Julie. You taught me that teachers have to always be prepared to think on their feet, or in their seats, or wherever they are, to answer their students' never-ending questions and help them make sense of their confusing world. After all, some of it, in their eyes, is quite awful.

Drew

Lillie, our school secretary, came to my classroom door and motioned me out into the hall. She had a manila folder in her hand, which signaled a new student.

As I joined her, I immediately thought there had been a mistake, although she rarely made one. The student standing beside her was tall—very tall—and he had lost the chubby baby cheeks that all my kindergarteners had. I could tell that not only had he lost his two front teeth, he had sprouted new ones.

The secretary, who over the years had learned to read my mind, hurried with his introduction. "Mrs. Rodgers, this is Drew Shane, and he is coming to us from West Virginia." She handed me his folder with her finger pointing to his birth date so she could non-verbally address the confusion on my face.

Doing the math in my head, I came up with a number that had to be incorrect, so I did it again. No, it came out the same. Drew was seven years old.

Giving me a smile that let me know she would talk to me later, she left me alone with my new student.

"Why, hello, Drew," I said cheerfully. "Come on in and we'll get you settled."

He followed obediently. The rest of the children were busy working in their centers, so it was a perfect time to introduce Drew to his classroom and to some of his classmates. First though, I needed to get his lunch situation squared away and label his cubby in our spacious walk-in closet.

"Drew, do you have lunch money with you or did you pack?" I asked routinely.

I was not prepared for his reply.

"Ah don av n e ting ta ea."

If what I have written is hard to read, believe me, it was twice as hard to understand.

I asked again, and his reply was exactly the same, although this time I forced myself to listen more closely. What I heard translated in my brain to mean, "I don't have anything to eat."

"Okay," I said. "Don't you worry about a thing. We'll get you a lunch and you'll love it. The cafeteria ladies here cook real well."

He smiled, then quietly changed to a more serious look. "I ungie ow," he replied.

I searched my brain. I didn't want to have to ask him to repeat everything he said, but I had to. I simply could not decipher yet, at least not on the first try.

He repeated, and like magic, I heard it loud and clear. "I'm hungry now."

I asked him if he had eaten breakfast, and he shook his head no. I glanced at the clock and knew that breakfast was no longer being served in our cafeteria, so I led him to my emergency cabinet. That's where I store clothes of every size, coats, boots, shoes, snuggly stuffed animals, extra book bags, and food.

I took out a loaf of bread and a jar of peanut butter, and in seconds Drew was happily feeding his grumbly tummy. While he was eating, I turned my attention to his folder, hoping it would offer answers to some of my mounting questions.

It seems Drew had started kindergarten later than usual. His parents had actually attempted to enroll him in first grade, but he was developmentally so far behind that he had been placed back in a kindergarten class. At the close of that year, he had not mastered the skill-set required to pass, so he was retained. Then his family moved here, and he was placed, once again, in kindergarten. Valuable time had already been lost. He was seven years old, but he had to complete and pass one full year at this level.

I turned back to Drew, who by now had finished his sandwich and was standing beside me.

"Ut dh uh ow?" he asked, and the only way I knew it was a question was the rise in inflection at the end.

I didn't ask him to repeat; I just replayed it in my head. When I pushed my internal play button, I heard, "What do I do now?"

"Come with me and I'll show you around," I replied, and thankfully my response seemed to satisfy his question.

I showed Drew the bathroom, the closet, and all the centers. We selected a desk, and I introduced him to his new classmates, one by one. He repeated each name, and by doing this he helped me "break his code," so to speak. I realized that he spoke in a staccato-note fashion, and because I have a musical background, I knew I could do this. He didn't stay on one word long enough to complete it—only one or two syllables of each word was touched on and then he was off to the next word. He had definite command of his language, and I would have to learn it in order to teach him mine.

Drew settled into his new surroundings like a square peg trying to squeeze into a round hole. He rarely mingled with the other children, choosing, rather, to stand at the end of the line and several feet back. It was as if standing close would only exaggerate the size difference. His class-mates fully accepted him and wanted to be friends, but Drew just seemed to prefer being alone.

I seemed to be the only one he wanted to talk to, and in the weeks and months ahead, we covered a lot of ground.

I was the only teacher in the school who could understand Drew, and I was working with him to improve his speech. Several teachers remarked that I was fluent in "DrewShananese," which was the label they had secretly given his language.

There was also another area of Drew's life I was beginning to understand better. He had a horrific home life. He was always hungry, and often I would put beanie weenies in his book bag for the evenings and weekends. Once, he and his sister came to school soaking wet. Seems their father had thrown them into the Smith River behind their house. Fearing they would be late getting to the school bus stop, they had refused to walk to the local store to pick up beer the storeowner had for their father. His angry response was to push them into the river.

Social Services, you may ask? Yes, they were called. Numerous times. Drew's case was reported to them. I have no answers as to why the cavalry did not come. He was always hungry, always dirty, and he missed school often.

Regardless, between the hunger, the abuse, the truancy, the neglect, and the humiliation of being a seven-year-old in a class of fives, Drew learned. He was attentive, well behaved, and extremely helpful to me. And he wanted to succeed. His language had improved by spring to the point where a few others could understand him.

About this time the C.A.P. Program was hitting the trash and S.O.L.s were being ushered in. Even at the kindergarten level, there were standardized tests that were designed around what somebody, somewhere, thought all five-year-olds should know. I had worked diligently all year trying to teach all I thought the children needed to know, along with what somebody else thought they needed to know.

Testing day was drawing near. Drew was the only one who kept asking about it. He was old enough to be worried and had probably already been harassed about it at home. He wanted to pass and move to a higher grade. We reviewed for days. Drew was absent on many of those days, but I tried to catch him up on the missed material.

The day came, and I had a helper in the classroom so I could test each child individually out in the hallway. Drew was pacing, knowing he would soon be called.

His turn came, and he angled his lanky body into the desk in the hallway. I was facing him and I could see his jaw set in determination. I smiled to assure him that all would be fine, and I patted his hand. "Drew, I'm going to tell you some important people, and you have to tell me three things you know about them. Do you understand?"

He nodded that he did.

"Okay, the first is Abraham Lincoln. Tell me three things you remember learning about him."

Drawing his body up tall and straight in his desk and pulling his arms up over his head to aid his description, Drew said, "E or a big 'tove pipe hat."

"Yes, he did, Drew. That's good." I was so pleased at how clear most of his words were.

"Ann he was 'ixteen pwesident of Oonited Tates."

"Yes Drew. That is correct."

"And he wa born n a og 'abin."

"Drew, that's correct! You are doing great."

I felt his enthusiasm as he sat beaming from ear to ear. He watched as I checked him off in the appropriate box.

"Okay, your next important person is George Washington. Tell me three things you know about him."

Drew wrinkled his brow for only a second, then he was off and running. "E wa da firs pwesident."

"Yes," I prodded him on. "What else?"

"E didn't tell wies."

"That's right. Now, just one more thing."

"E wuz n da awmee.

"Yes, Drew! That's great." I made the checkmark extra big so he could see it.

He radiated jubilation.

"Okay, Drew. We're almost done with our social studies test. You just have one more person. "Tell me three things about Thomas Jefferson."

The look on his face was a mix of "deer in the headlights" and "I've just lost my best friend." As he struggled, his body shifted side to side in his desk. My own mind raced back over the days we had studied Jefferson. Had

Drew been absent on those days? Had I reviewed him enough? We had certainly covered all the material on this equally important historical figure.

Drew glanced at me briefly, and I saw him mouthing the words "Thomas Jefferson," as if that would jog his memory. His bewildered look changed to something that resembled fear. His fighting took over his whole body as his fingers started drumming the desk. Then, as if pleading for me to end his pain, he shouted, "Who da hell iz dat?"

My eyes met his. I saw a child who came to school hungry every day and would leave in the afternoon looking forward to coming back. I saw a child who, for whatever reason, was delayed in his academic progress but was doing everything he could to catch up. I saw a child whose father would throw him in the river if he refused to bring him beer.

I looked again at his eyes as he searched mine for an answer.

"That's okay, Drew. You've already passed your test. Fantastic job," I said as I checked off the last box. I saw gratitude and relief cross his face.

Drew Shane, you taught a budding teacher that we should always look at the big picture instead of all the little boxes. It's *that* picture that paints a thousand words.

Kasey P.

Throughout my teaching career, it has been my practice to develop behavioral modifications to handle the active and/or inattentive students who came into my classroom. They are not much older than toddlers—between the ages of four and six—and I do not believe in seeking medication for these children. According to FDA guidelines, behavior modifications are recommended for children under the age of six. So when parents come to me asking that I please help them keep their child from going down the medical route of diagnosing and being sedated, I am all too willing to oblige. After all, I consider it my job, not a pill's, to find the method that works in the classroom. It's the parent's job, not mine, to find what works at home. Solid success is reached when we work together. That produces results. Such was the case with Kasey.

I knew his family well. Their older son was already attending this elementary school. A model student, bright, helpful, and mannerly.

On registration day, Kasey's parents shook their heads and offered apologies and condolences. "Kasey," they said, "is more active than our older son."

"That's fine," I responded. "That way I can tell them apart."

They reported that Kasey was impulsive, hardheaded, strong-willed, and active. They also added that he was loving, smart, imaginative, and inquisitive. They promised to help me out with his behavior in the classroom. Like me, they did not believe in medication. We made a pact, then and there, to never mention pills when speaking of Kasey. I was to call them whenever Kasey's behavior became disruptive and he was unresponsive to my classroom management plan. His father would leave work and come to handle the situation.

Everything Kasey's parents reported about him was accurate. They had observed and labeled his behaviors well. However, there was one attribute, for some unknown reason, they forgot to mention to me. They never shared how hysterically funny Kasey was.

We were seated at the tables, getting ready to have snacks on our first day of school. There were two, kidney-shaped tables in my classroom, seating eight students each. I sit in the center of one and my assistant at the other. I had purposely assigned Kasey to sit beside me.

As I watched him enjoying his snack, I couldn't help but think how cute he was. I was already thinking ahead to my Christmas play. Kasey would be an elf for sure. He was a wiry child with brown hair and pointy features. He was a dead ringer for Hermie, the dentist in *Rudolf the Red Nosed Reindeer*. As Kasey sat there, I noticed that he stopped eating and lay down his peanut-butter cracker.

He sat motionless for a moment as if he considering something in his deepest thoughts. Then he spoke in his cute Southern drawl. "Mrs. Roodgerrrs," he said, dragging out every syllable. "If I wuz a dog, I'd pee on a tree."

"Oh, you would?" I asked, amused. "Well, you're not a doggie, you're a little boy, and little boys pee in the bathroom. Do you need to use the bathroom?"

He nodded a bit frantically.

"Well, let me show you where it is." I led him to our classroom restroom.

We never knew what Kasey was going to say or do, but you could be assured it would elicit laughter.

On another day, we were all busy in centers, and my assistant and I were making our rounds, offering help as needed. There had been a stomach virus rearing its ugly head in our classroom, and several children were obviously coming down with symptoms. Our little bathroom seemed to be a hot spot. After one child went in, even though the door was tightly closed, the very unpleasant odor of a lower GI problem filled the room. Kasey went dashing to my shelf where I keep my sprays and soaps, grabbed the deodorizer, and started spraying under the door, the whole time yelling, "Fire in the hole! Fire in the hole!"

There were countless other knee-slapping antics, but by far the most amusing came during language arts one day. I had developed a most effective method for teaching beginning sounds. I first introduced the letter, writing it on my large chart tablet. After the children heard the sound several times, they tried to come up with things that began with that particular sound. I then drew it on the paper and wrote the word under it. There were several instructional lessons going on simultaneously. They heard the sound, saw creativity in drawing, and saw the word in print. Then we had a permanent book of pictures and letter sounds to review. Children have told me they learned to draw by watching me create the pictures from start to finish. So much more imaginative than simply clicking a picture on a computer or active board. And the children had a part in creating it, so they had better recall.

This day, we were learning the letter W. I had already gone through the initial steps and now awaited ideas from the children. "Wagon," said one student, and I magically created a wagon on the board.

"Watermelon," said another, and I drew the familiar fruit with ease.

Several other children added to my growing collage of pictures. Kasey, however, was struggling. He often had trouble with this activity, no matter how much effort he put into it. He could distinguish the difference in sounds and could even sort picture cards into appropriate letter piles. But coming up with the object first was sometimes difficult. I could see him mouthing the W sound over and over, trying to think of something. He wanted so badly to raise his hand. Suddenly, he jumped up and blurted out, "One-eyed Willie!"

The shock on my assistant's face was priceless. The shock on my face, however, came with a price tag. I had to recover from this one.

My assistant, covering her face as she headed quickly away, passed by me and whispered, "Let's see you draw this one!"

Trying to stifle my laughter, I began my cover-up. "Well, Kasey, very good. You've come up with something that does indeed have the W sound." From the proud look on Kasey's face, and the nonchalant look on all the others' faces, I guessed that no one in the room other than myself and Miss Domica knew what a "one-eyed Willie" referred to. I had to continue. They were all waiting for the picture.

"But there's a problem with the word. It has the W sound but actually begins with an O. One is spelled o-n-e, so I can't use that idea, Kasey, I'm sorry."

In order to help him save face, I gave him a few hints to name the bird I knew he could hear calling at nighttime at his house. He shouted, "Whippoorwill," and I happily drew the tiny bird.

My assistant, Miss Domica, and I had to take a break in the corner of the room and laugh until our bellies hurt.

Fire in the hole, one-eyed Willie, and peeing on a tree aside, Kasey had a successful pre-k year. He learned all the skills he needed to advance to kindergarten. His behavior at times was disruptive, but with the help of his parents, was manageable. He was a joy to have in my classroom, and I shudder to think what everyone would have missed if he had been sedated and lethargic. I learned through Kasey to continue sticking to my convictions and giving parents backup when they wanted to stick to theirs.

Trevor

He was a powerhouse of personality. Big, flashy smile that he showed off every time I looked at him. Chocolate-brown eyes that reminded me of my favorite truffles. Everyone loved Trevor. He found something to laugh about *and* make everyone else laugh when no one else could. Being the youngest of three boys, he had certainly mastered making a name for himself.

And now, let's talk about lesson plans. Teachers have to write them. Administration requires them. But I personally never, *ever* saw the usefulness of them. I could always teach an effective, well-planned lesson without all the hullabaloo of writing it all down first. I had a mental inventory of what children needed to learn, the materials needed to teach it, and the process of getting that done effectively. My daily lessons flowed like an age-old creek, with me never having to look at my plan book. I would write the things, file them for review, and the book would stay closed until I was required to do more. I preferred to stay tuned in to the needs of the class each day. I would often change my plan on a second's notice, especially after I arrived at school and realized the students were in need of another lesson more than the one that had previously been written for the day. Nevertheless, my superiors specifically required that everything in a lesson be written down. It didn't matter if you had it in your head. *All* materials, word for word what I said, *all* of it had to be written down. Seemed like a waste of time to me. But every profession has protocol.

Then came the day I learned *my* lesson. I had been up all night with two sick children and knew I would need a substitute for the next day. Attempting to hurry along my lesson plans for my stand-in, I left notes to have a few children help her out. Bailey would know where the art supplies were. Chester could show her where the playground balls and jump ropes were. And Trevor could certainly lead the music. He knew all the songs, could sing like Michael Jackson, and didn't have a shy bone in his body. Yes, I was confident I could just skip all the details and write those children's names beside the activity.

Imagine my surprise when I arrived at school the day following my absence, and there was a note at the top of my plans, written in bright red highlighter, "SEE ME, PLEASE."

The substitute who had been assigned to my class was actually subbing for another teacher in the school that day, so I hurried to see her. A dozen scenarios were flashing through my head. What had happened?

She smiled when I entered the room, and she began to recant the day before. All had gone smoothly with the early morning routine. But . . . then came music. She had called Trevor to the front to lead the class in the songs we had learned. He had happily taken center stage at the front and beamed with joy at his good fortune of being chosen for the task. When the substitute told him he could begin, he had immediately broken out in a hip-swinging, finger-snapping, arm-swaying rendition of "Do a little dance, Make a little love, Get down tonight, Get down tonight."

Horrified, the substitute had stopped him at the last "Get down tonight" and inquired if Mrs. Rodgers had indeed taught that song to them?

Trevor had meekly replied, "No, ma'am," and he was instructed to lead the class in an appropriate song. He then proceeded with a not-so-soulful "Six Little Ducks."

Ohhh, my little Trevor. You indeed taught me the need for *detailed* lesson plans for *all* my substitutes.

Mackensie

She was adorable. Coffee-with-cream skin, dark hair that was always in perfect braids, and a shy little smile that could melt your heart. She did the neatest work and was *always* perfectly behaved. I never had to reprimand her for talking during lessons or for disruptions during centers or playtime. She never ran in the hallway or climbed on the railings. Sometimes, I found myself worrying that she was *too* good. I mean, she was only five years old. I expect an occasional bout of unruliness at that age; I even think it's good for them. But not Mackensie. She didn't even tattle on the other children when they were being unruly enough for the both of them.

Then came the Monday morning when Mackensie showed up to school with a small cut across her forehead, some bruises on her cheeks, and some Band-Aids on her knees. I immediately called her up to my desk to get to the bottom of what had happened to my little angel. "Mackensie! What in the world happened to you? You have so many booboos."

"I got hurt at church," was her soft-spoken reply.

"Hurt at church?" My mind was reeling with all the possible scenarios. Had Mackensie been running through the halls? Was she sliding down the banister? Had she gotten into a ruckus with some of her little friends? Had she finally "broken bad" and behaved like a normal five year old? I smiled to myself just thinking of that possibility. So, I had to ask, "Mackensie, were you running at church?"

"No, ma'am. Miss Bishop was standing next to me and she got the spirit and fell over on top of me and I hit the pew and landed real hard on the floor."

She looked me straight in the face with such serenity that it would have been impossible to doubt a single word of it. And I was left with the mental image of this tiny little girl, dressed in her Sunday finest, lying in a heap on the church floor with a spirit-filled parishioner on top of her.

Oh, little Mackensie. She taught me that even if you're doing everything you can to be good, if the person you're close to gets the spirit, either good or bad, you just might get the ripple effect.

Tucker

This is one of those stories that no one wants to ever hear or read about. I came very close to not even including it in my book. Yet Tucker, his brother, and their mother were a very real part of my life. And when you choose teaching as a career, you are accepting the risk of experiencing your students' tragedies. You may also discover that you are the only one to help a mother through the worst nightmare imaginable.

Tucker was a student who didn't really stand out for any particular reason. He didn't excel in any academic area but wasn't struggling, either. There were a few notes sent home for his mother to help him review some of the kindergarten skills, and she always would.

Tucker loved to draw and I encouraged that. He didn't talk very much, and sometimes, I would wonder if something was heavy on his mind. Drawing seemed to give him an outlet for expression.

He and his younger brother looked so much alike that they could have easily passed for twins. Both had sandy blond hair and a big splash of tan freckles across their noses. I thought they looked just like their mom but realized I had never met their dad.

Tucker's little brother was in the pre-k class at the same school, and I would see them wave at each other at lunch and on the playground. Tucker definitely played the part of protective big brother.

Toward the middle of the school year, Tucker began being absent or tardy much of the time. Then came the day his mother brought him to the door of the room, and her eyes were bruised and swollen, noticeable even behind her dark glasses. I could tell she was visibly upset. Following my instincts, I sent Tucker into the classroom and stood with his mom just outside the door. I asked her if she was okay and if I could help in any way.

Her pain poured out. Her husband was an alcoholic and abusive. She feared for her life but had been staying in the home because she didn't want the boys to ever be with him alone. Now the physical abuse was so bad that she knew she would be killed if she stayed. She had made the decision to leave him. The future horrified her. The past haunted her. The present threatened her.

She left in tears and I slipped back into my classroom to see if Tucker needed comforting. It had obviously been a stressful morning for the entire family.

The next morning brought another tearful visit. Tucker, his brother, and their mother were now at a different residence. There would be a custody hearing and, ultimately, a divorce. I will never forget how her voice trembled as she poured out her deepest fear. "I just know something is going to happen to my boys when they're with him. By law, he will be getting visitation with them every other weekend." Her attorney had warned her that the law upheld the parents' rights to a child above all else. And the father was also their parent, regardless of how bad a parent he was.

I could feel her anguish. She felt guilty for leaving the situation that threatened her with certain death yet opened the door for her husband to have the boys without her constant protection.

During the month leading up to the father's first unsupervised visitation, Tucker, his brother, and their mother had begun to show signs of healing. She started looking rested, the boys were smiling, looked clean, and arrived at school on time every day. I was hopeful that things were finally going to settle down for this little family.

But then the Friday arrived when the dad would be getting the boys after school. Their mother brought Tucker and his brother to my classroom door. Tears welled in her eyes. "Their father has his first weekend with them," she said. "I will pace the floor. I am so scared." She hugged Tucker and left him with me. Then she led his brother to his pre-k classroom. That was to be the last time she would ever see her youngest alive.

That very evening, the father ran a stop sign. He was so intoxicated that he never applied the brakes. The father, his youngest son, and the driver of the other vehicle all died at the scene. Tucker was airlifted to the nearest trauma center.

I read about the accident in the local Sunday newspaper. By afternoon, my principal and the other teachers were calling me. I found out that Tucker was in a coma. My heart turned to his mother. I knew I should go to her.

She was sitting beside his bed with her head resting on his pillow and her arm across his chest. The only part of Tucker's body that was visible was his closed eyes. His entire body was wrapped in casting bandages, and all of his limbs were held up in traction. It was a gut-wrenching, unspeakable scene.

I don't recall much of our conversation, except for the words, "I knew this was going to happen. I wish it had happened to me."

I hugged her and could feel her anguished sobs.

Tucker remained in the hospital in a coma for six months. Then he was transported to a rehabilitation center where he had to learn how to move again. During this time, I visited them and talked to his mother often on the phone. She was in a constant state of grief, loss, and guilt. I recall telling her that she had been spared so she could take care of Tucker. She found comfort in that and devoted her life to being there for him.

The lesson from Tucker is a troubling one. It was an awareness of how fragile life is. His situation also uncovered a tragic flaw in our judicial system. Sometimes, when the law "upholds the parents' rights to a child above all else," it shouldn't.

Billy

I noticed right away, on the very first day of school, that he was active. He also liked to make friends with everybody, not just those seated near him.

Billy was above average in size for a preschooler. Tall, athletic looking, and a very animated face. He used his eyes to emphasize his words, his mouth would scrunch his cheeks to one side, and he'd even twitch his nose on occasion. I knew right away I was going to enjoy Billy's antics and his conversations.

He loved to talk about his family. They obviously did a lot together, and he always had stories to tell about their adventures. But school was definitely going to crimp Billy's style. He was a mover and a shaker, and I don't think there had been any events in his young life where he had been required to sit still for anything.

So it was going to be my task to ease Billy into sitting still long enough to listen to stories and practice his coloring and other pre-k skills we would be working on. My daily schedule allowed for a lot of movement, but Billy didn't appear to think it was enough. He would pop right out of his seat like it was on fire. And when he popped up, his legs would immediately take him over to a friend so he could start up one of those animated conversations.

I realized quite quickly that Billy just liked to be in close proximity to others. He was accustomed to the security of having his family close by. Now, here at school, he just wanted to continue the togetherness by scrunching up close to his new little friends. And while that is an endearing attribute, I was faced with maintaining the other children's personal space while they did their work. I knew I had my task cut out for me; I feel it's our job as teachers to break certain habits while not breaking spirits.

So I watched and waited. I knew the answer would come to me . . . and it did.

One day while we were doing art, I was walking about the room assisting the children as needed. Billy had been instructed to stay in his area for the twenty minutes we were doing our "creative expression." I realized we were well into the timeframe, and Billy had not left his seat. He was happily working, and there had been no darting about the room or interrupting the other children.

I walked over to Billy's workspace, and as I got closer, I heard him whispering. When I was beside him, I saw who he was conversing with. Arranged all around his space were beautifully made construction-paper people. It was absolutely delightful. I inquired who they were, and he named each one, stating, with a smile, "This is my family!"

So there was the answer to our "keep Billy in his seat for a while" dilemma.

Each day after that, during times when Billy had to remain seated for story time, seatwork, art, or a lesson, he was allowed to retrieve his "family," and they all sat with him. Gradually, the quick flights about the room decreased, and Billy saw that he was never really alone in our little classroom. Billy, once again, confirmed my passion to "break little habits" without "breaking big spirits."

Adalie

I will always think of her as my very last student. Even though I had sixteen that year, just like all my pre-k years, she will forever be the "last" one. In a way, she symbolized all I taught for, fought for, loved and grieved for during my teaching career.

She was like a little elf—or maybe, a fairy. Tiny framed, brown curly ringlets falling around her shoulders, and eyes that sparkled like pixie dust. She loved everything about coming to school.

Each day, she was the first one to arrive. Her mother was a teacher at the school, so Adalie would usually see me in the office as we checked in. She couldn't wait to run to me and ask in her bubbly way, "What are we going to do today?" Often she would pass me pictures or notes she had done for me the evening before.

Adalie loved everything we did. She eagerly awaited the pledge, which she recited loud and clear. She proudly stood at attention and faced the flag. Often, I would steal a glance at her with her head thrown back, right hand over her heart, eyes fixed on the Stars and Stripes. Following the pledge was a moment of silence. Her eyes were always closed, head bowed, and hands folded together in the unashamed attitude of prayer.

Academics were tackled with great appreciation. She loved hearing stories, learning letters and sounds, and experimenting with reading and writing words. She looked forward to centers, and on most days, she headed to the art table. I had boxes of buttons and material scraps, markers and paper, crayons and paints, glue, glitter, and tape. She created elaborate hats, clothes, collages, and books. Her designs were amazing.

I always cooked with my classes on Thursdays. Adalie would just wiggle with excitement. Sometimes, she would ask for the recipes so she could do a repeat of the lesson at home.

But as much as she loved all the activities I've mentioned, her favorite was music, and just like the old McLean song, "American Pie," it was Adalie who shared a tear with me "the day the music died."

I love music. I was born and raised to flat-footin' bluegrass, always around somebody playing something. At age seven, I started playing the piano and took lessons well into my high school years. I became church pianist at age sixteen and continued until my fifties. I remember a professor in college telling me to always share my music with my students, that it was a gift and also a method of teaching. He said that singing songs helps children with rhythm, rhyming, language development, and creativity. I followed his advice and had a piano in my room for most of my teaching career.

The children just loved it. Gathering around the piano every morning grew to be the highlight of the day. I have quite the foot-stomping style of playing, and the children ended up clapping their hands and patting their feet to the rhythm of the music.

Adalie just became lost in the songs. She loved it so much. If there was an assembly, or even a field trip that took up the usual morning schedule, she always asked, "Are we going to have music?" I tried to work it in if at all possible.

As this particular school year drew to a close, I also began to realize that my teaching career was likewise in its final days. Over my thirty-one years of teaching, I had seen many changes in education. While a few of them were good—and even necessary—for the most part I did not see some of the changes as being beneficial to the children. Computers were rapidly replacing the teacher in the classroom. Creativity was being replaced by curriculum guides and pacing calendars. Teaching children morals and discipline, and simply right from wrong, was overshadowed by self-esteem choices and self-expression programs. I had declined repeated offers for a costly active board in my classroom. Preferring to use inexpensive, creative instructional tools such as a chalkboard, chart tablets, and dry-erase boards, I found myself facing hard opposition. I was going to be required to put iPads in the hands of four-year-olds when I felt that, developmentally, they should be holding blocks, Play-Doh, and paintbrushes. It was heartbreaking for me to see active children being sedated at an alarming rate because they couldn't sit still.

I was beginning to realize that my teaching style was not acceptable by the new cookie-cutter method. Active boards were used to bring whatever music or dancing exposure into the classroom the curriculum allowed. The push was on to have all teachers at each grade level doing the same thing, the same way. A week before the end of the school year, the piano was wheeled out of my classroom.

Adalie was the one who led the others in their cries. "Mrs. Rodgers," she wailed, "where are they taking your piano? We won't be able to sing our songs anymore!" She was sobbing so hard that her words were barely audible.

I tried to console her. "Adalie, we can use some cassettes or sing by ourselves. Or we can sing along with some music videos on the active board."

What she said next just solidified my decision to retire. "Mrs. Rodgers, when you play the piano, it's bumpy and wiggly." She demonstrated with a wiggle of her hips and a few flips of her hands, tossing her wild hair back and forth. "But when we listen to the tapes, it's all flat!" Again, she demonstrated with palms flat, moving back and forth as if following a straight line in front of her. Her eyes were sad and the last of her tears streamed down her face.

I followed my piano down the hall, stopped by the office, and filled out my resignation forms.

Oh, my Adalie, my sweet, wise-beyond-your-years Adalie. The lessons you taught weren't just for me but for all those who can't see that education is supposed to be wiggly and bumpy and full of all kinds of songs. After all, the world is not flat.

Somebody proved that . . . a very long time ago.

LOST SONG

I can't believe I sing alone
My song is good, my voice is strong
I try so hard to teach the words
So all who hear will sing along.

But all they hear is their own tune
They like their voice, their words they croon
They teach theirs is the only song
They are right, and I am wrong.

There was a time when voices rose
Around the world, together clear
All shared a song, all shared a dream
And now . . . it's wrong to sing, it seems.

It's wrong to sing of what is right
To shun the dark, to walk in light.
To nourish souls is not their dream
And their tune is loud, their voices scream.

And screams are heard above a song
And one by one others scream along
Until the old tunes fade away
And singing dies . . . but screaming stays.

And hope seems lost, and faith seems old
So little children are seldom told
That from their souls, a song can ring
And from these songs, learning brings.

But others choose to glare at faces
Sedate their smiles, confine their spaces
To cubicles without the sun
No open fields where children run.

And learning has to come from boxes
With wires and plugs and heartless croxes
'Til eyes with lights are reduced to stares
And blankness is the stare they share.

It makes me want to sing much louder
To rise above the horrid voices
That takes away a small child's right
To learn what's right . . . to make right
choices.

Oh . . . my heart is heavy.
My soul does moan
I can't believe I sing alone.

~Betsy Henny 2012

After Class

My teaching career spanned thirty-one years and three elementary schools in two neighboring counties. I was fortunate in that this situation alone allowed me to know my children's extended families. Additionally, any outing to the grocery store, post office, mall, hair salon, virtually *anywhere* found me running into former students and their relatives.

I have had numerous reconnections with some of my Little Teachers. Even though they are grown now, and I even taught a few of their children, I still see the little pre-k or kindergarten child who became part of my life so many years ago. I cannot imagine any other profession that allows one to have such a profound connection with the life and the future of another.

Following are just a few of the reconnections I experienced. I hope you find these stories—and the ones already told—inspirational.

Kasey H.

I was heading to the entrance of the local grocery store when I heard someone calling my name. Turning, I saw a teenage girl walking toward me, smiling. "Mrs. Rodgers! Do you remember me?" she excitedly asked.

I certainly did. Her face had not changed a bit. But before I could reply, she answered her own question.

"It's Kasey! Remember how bad I was? I'm not bad anymore!"

I was laughing by this time and opened my arms wide for a hug. "Kasey, you weren't bad. Just full of yourself." I fondly added, "What are you doing now, young lady?"

"I'm getting ready to go to college," she said, just bubbling. "I'm probably going to do mission work!"

I listened while this beautiful girl caught me up on her life. She had made exceptional grades in high school, was active in her community and church, and even did theater work.

"Thank you for not giving up on me, Mrs. Rodgers," she said as she gave me one more hug. "I can't believe how mean I was."

As we parted ways, I had to laugh to myself. How lovely that she had chosen mission work over going to hell to see the devil!

Micah

It is such a joy to see this little guy. From not being able to speak or drink from a cup to reading and performing above-grade-level work . . . he had covered a lot of ground. His mother had been steadily devoted and part of his progress. I always sought him out whenever I subbed at his elementary school. I could understand every word perfectly, he had lots of friends, and there was always a smile on his face.

Kacey

I was going to the office to retrieve my attendance sheet and mail. As I entered the lobby area, a striking red-headed woman stopped me. "Mrs. Rodgers, I don't know if you remember me or not, but you were my kindergarten teacher."

Immediately, my eyes met hers and I knew. "Kacey!" I said affirmatively and pulled her in for an endearing embrace. I had not laid eyes on her since kindergarten.

Briefly, she gave me the highlights with a promise to sit down and really talk when we had time. She was married and now working at the school as part of Family Preservation. She and her sister had taken her daddy's last name and had attended a private school following her year with me. That's why I had completely lost track of her.

She recalled that school year and told me that she had been so attached to me after losing her mother. She said, "I remember you rocking me in your rocking chair every day. That always made me feel so much better."

The next day, I received a lovely email from her, again thanking me for helping her through the toughest year of her life.

I returned her email with a note of appreciation to her. Those sessions in the rocking chair taught me to treasure what is truly precious in life. Her mother's love rained down from heaven on both of us as we daily rocked in that rocking chair.

As I am writing this, I just had a fabulous idea. I'm going to the storage unit and retrieve that rocking chair. What a perfect gift for Kacey as she awaits the adoption of her new baby.

I'm certain her mother would approve.

Leah

I had just loaded my kids on their buses and was headed back to straighten my room and prepare for the next day. A woman was leaving the office with two children in tow. She smiled at me as though she wanted to say something. When I returned the smile, she took the opportunity to speak. "Mrs. Rodgers, you were my kindergarten teacher and I just loved you. Do you remember me?"

Minus the waist-length hair, she looked exactly the same. "Leah," I said warmly. " Oh gracious!"

We embraced and just stood there, both of us probably thinking the same thing. I was remembering just how many times I had hugged her, and even though twenty-seven years had passed, it still felt the same. It felt like hugging family.

We stood there in the lobby and talked. My very first student was now the mother of two. The youngest was pre-school age, and she had heard I was the teacher at this school.

"I've been wanting to get a job in the school system," she said, "but I just couldn't think of sending Tanner to preschool . . . until I heard you taught here. Now I'm going to enroll him. You're the only one I would trust him with."

And so began a rekindled friendship and bond on an entirely different level. Teaching children of children you've taught is much like having grandchildren. It's like seeing all the love, blood, sweat, and tears that you poured into one human being spilling out into another.

It's definitely the icing on an already good cake.

Stephanie

I was ordering a sandwich from Subway. This is probably one of the most ordinary, commonplace things one can do in a day. Yet the routine turned into the unexpected as the young girl taking my order asked me an unusual question.

"Have you saved any more lives lately?"

I was digging in my purse for my wallet but stopped instantly and looked at her with greater scrutiny. I was stumped. I honestly did not know what she was talking about. She saw my hesitation and confusion.

"I'm Stephanie. You saved my life in kindergarten. I wasn't in your class, but you unchoked me when I swallowed a marble."

Of course I remembered her as soon as she said her name.

We couldn't chat while hungry patrons were in line behind me, so I took a seat in a booth and Stephanie joined me during her break.

She was attending a college in a nearby city, studying to be a preacher. Working at Subway was helping pay her tuition. "Just think," she told me. "That day I was choking

I thought I was going to see Jesus. Now I'm going to school to spread His word."

Isn't it heartwarming what some people do with second chances?

Sadie

She was one who left my classroom but never left me. Every single morning, she would head straight to give me a huge hug. Her beloved papa drove her to school and picked her up in the afternoon. This is the same grandfather who flat-footed for me in order to bribe entry for Sadie into pre-k. He was her world.

Then one day, he was gone. He died suddenly and left a little girl with a broken heart. Sadie wrapped her arms around me at the funeral home, and I could feel her sobs.

After this, my mornings were a bit longer than before. It took me a few more minutes to get her usual smile. I would look for her in the cafeteria to make sure she was eating. I had noticed she had been throwing her entire breakfast and lunch away. I made a point to ask her daily how she was doing and if she needed to talk. Slowly, her heart began to go through the healing process and her smiles returned.

It was such a special time—my morning hugs from Sadie. But then word traveled concerning my retirement plans. I will forever remember Sadie confronting me with the question that would weigh heavy on my heart.

She came walking straight to me, and stopping just inches away, she locked her eyes on mine. "So, just tell me one thing. Just who is going to hug me every day?"

I just hate it when I can't answer a question. And this was one I couldn't respond definitely to. I did hug her and tell her that I would be subbing as often as I could. And I promised to find her and catch up on all the missed hugs whenever I came back.

It is a promise I have kept.

Lamar

I don't go to malls much, especially during the Christmas season. I prefer to either make my gifts or shop specialty stores throughout the year. If I go to a mall during the busy holiday season, it's just to see the sights. I love to people watch and take in all the music and decorations.

Such was the case this particular day. I was just strolling and looking when I heard my name called . . . very loudly! I turned to see a young man in his early twenties walking toward me. He was wearing sagging jeans and an oversized jersey and had corn-rowed hair. And he was grinning from ear to ear. When he got close enough to me, he picked me up and twirled me around.

"Do you remember me?" he boomed loud enough for the entire Christmas crowd to hear him. "I'm Lamar! You taught me how to tie my shoes."

Well, I couldn't help myself. I had to look down. His shoelaces were sprawled in an untidy mess all around his sneakers.

He glanced down, too, and laughed. "Well, you taught me. I just don't do it now. It's the style, you know."

We laughed and talked and he showed me pictures of his beautiful boys.

It was so good to see him. We talked a few more minutes, then hugged one more time and parted ways.

It was sometime the following summer when I heard of Lamar again. The secretary from the school, who has been my best friend from my first day of teaching, called me. "Betsy, did you see where Lamar has been arrested?"

"No way," I cried. "Whatever for?"

Well, it seems the local radio station sent their racist news reporter to an incident on Lamar's street. He spouted off at Lamar in a string of racial slurs and Lamar punched him in the jaw.

"Betsy! Let's go bail Lamar out so he can go finish beating him up," she implored.

We seriously considered it. We just loved Lamar.

And after all . . . we knew the reporter didn't have manners, and very likely, he didn't even say "please."

Kasey P.

Not many teachers can say they rounded up cows with one of their former students, but I can.

I was sitting in my den one evening when my German Shepherd bolted for the door, barking wildly. I looked out the window to see one of the cows headed across the front yard straight for the road.

I bolted, just like the dog, straight out the front door. The old black cow, persnickety as they come, was running blindly straight down the road. I crossed my gravel drive in hot pursuit. As I left the edge of the yard, I became aware of a car stopping in my driveway.

"Betsy, do you need any help?" came a voice from the car. I turned back to see Kasey's mom calling to me from her car window.

"I think I've got it," I yelled back, "but thank you."

I grabbed the nearest stick. Upon seeing that, the old cow had a change in "flight plans" and headed back toward the fenced pasture. It was at that moment that I saw the magnitude of the problem. The gate was wide open, and all twenty-seven cows were grazing in my back yard.

Kasey's mom saw it too. As she jumped from the car, I saw Kasey right behind her. He smiled at me and yelled, "I'll help you, Mrs. Rodgers."

So began our evening of cattle rustling. Kasey was a huge help, manning the gate, opening and closing it, as one by one the ornery cows lost their newfound freedom.

After the excitement was over, I had the chance to catch up with Kasey and his mom. They had met some opposition with their "no medication" conviction, so the decision had been made to enroll Kasey in a private school. He was thriving and his performance and grades were excellent—all in the absence of medication. That made me so happy. I could still see Kasey's "fire in the hole" spirit. That spirit certainly came in handy with a herd of ornery cows.

Jason

After my engagement to little Jason fell through, and the diamond was safely back on his mother's finger, life returned to normal, at least for a while. Jason and his brother finished pre-k and went on to complete six more years at the little elementary school.

During their final two years, their mother bravely fought cancer. She drove the school bus as long as she could. As the disease weakened her, she finally had to give that up but continued to be a help to the school in other capacities. She was one of those people everyone loves. Likewise, her love for others reflected in everything she did.

When she finally did slip away from us, she still had the last word. Her bus, in which she drove the children she loved to school each day, was the same bus all the teachers rode in to her funeral. Her eulogy was beautiful, eloquently prepared and delivered by her pastor. But the most beautiful words were written by Jennifer herself and read in the closing: The entire community was thanked and entrusted with her beautiful boys.

As I had previously shared my faith with her, so she

shared hers with me and all who knew her. She faced death with the same courage, faith, love, and humor with which she embraced life.

Her boys are living legacies to that spirit.

Hanna

There are some children who come with strings attached. These strings are connected to your heart, and no matter the miles or the years between, you will forever feel the tug.

Hanna's situation haunted me then and haunts me still. She was just so adorable and loving . . . and active. After leaving pre-k, she was heavily medicated, and the metamorphic deteriorative process began. I would see her walking the halls, sullen and depressed. She never made eye contact. Her clothes were dirty and never fit. I frequented the local thrift stores, purchased clothes for her, and took them by her house. Miss Domica and I sought her out to talk to her and try to find the Hanna we knew hidden somewhere inside.

After retirement I made it a point to look for Hanna whenever I subbed. I happened to be in her class the day before her fifth-grade dance. My heart broke for her as I heard all the other girls chatting about their new bows, frills, and shoes they would be wearing.

I made an afternoon trip to the Goodwill and found not just one beautiful dress but several. Also, outfits to see her through the end of school. There were even accessories to help her dress to impress. The gratitude and squeals from Hanna the next day warmed my heart. She looked beautiful as I watched her dancing and even saw the smiles I remembered.

I wish I could write something that would offer readers a more positive picture of Hanna's future. I cannot. Hanna's true problem is not being addressed. She is just being medicated to paint over the problem with a different color. A color that will blend instead of standing out.

These children who have strings attached . . . they are actually lifelines. And teachers everywhere need to grab hold and hold on—and remember to pull them in when they start sinking.

Billy

It was a beautiful October afternoon. I had happily returned to my last elementary school for a first-grade-substitute position. The children were frolicking on the playground like wild things let loose. I was seated on the bench and chatting with a few of my former students. It was so wonderful to see them again, see how they had grown, and hear what was going on in their lives.

A lot had changed in my life since I had last been to the school. I had remarried and was also a grandmother now. The new students, who were unfamiliar with my former last name, had no difficulty learning my new title as Mrs. Henny. All my previous students, however, kept having slip-ups, and I was usually addressed as "Mrs. Rodgers-uh-I-mean-Henny!"

As I sat there on the playground bench, I saw one of my former pre-k children in another class pick up the pace as he saw me from a distance. One of his buddies who was in my class that day tried to intercept him and herd him to the swing set. I overheard my former student say, "Hey! There's Mrs. Rodgers. I want to go see her!"

His friend informingly announced, "Her name is *Mrs.*

Henny now, but don't worry, she's still in there."

Bobbie Jo

After teaching pre-k and kindergarten for thirty-one years, I am still amazed at the far-reaching bonds that are made between student and teacher. Over the years, I have had former students rush to my side as paramedics, answer 911 calls as firefighters, fill my prescriptions, start my IV line in the ER, pull my car out of the ditch, give me a relaxing pedicure at the salon, and the list goes on.

And on this particular morning, I looked into the eyes of a former student, Bobbie Jo, as she joined the ever-growing circle of caretakers for my sweet mama. What a joyous moment we shared as we hugged and cried. For a brief, few seconds, she was once again that little five year old who I taught how to color, tie shoes, write her ABCs, share toys, *and* not lie about taking a classmate's lipstick. I had not seen her since kindergarten, but it was as if there had been no time apart.

I am so thankful that God led me into a career that allowed me to share the lives, families, and souls of children. I recall that every year, as I met a new group of students, I would reassure their parents by telling them that I promised to love and treat their babies exactly how I would want someone to love and treat my own.

I never imagined the ripple effect that promise would have until decades later. As it happened that Bobbie Jo was sitting with my sister and me, holding Mama's hand as she left this world and entered heaven.

I believe firmly that nothing happens by chance.

Anthony

I had quickly adjusted to my new elementary school. A few of the teachers I had worked with at my previous school were also at this assignment. It was much bigger than I was used to, housing four to five classrooms for each grade.

I was still teaching kindergarten. There were several special ed classrooms at the end of the hall nearest the office. Due to the different schedule of the kindergarten through second-grade classes, I rarely saw any of the special ed children on the playground or in the lunchroom. It wasn't like my old school where the departments had a lot of interaction.

As the end of the year approached, the special education teachers asked if any of the lower grades would like a helper to do any odd jobs to prepare for the end of the year. They were looking to give their older students, who qualified, a chance to leave their classroom for an hour and be a teacher's helper. I quickly volunteered, as I could sure use the help in taking down student work from the hallways.

After lunch that day, there was a knock on the door, and I saw the special ed aide through the small window. I hurried to open the door, and there, standing beside her, was Anthony. Same face, same glare, but now he was face to face with me. I would guess he was about twelve years old.

Neither the aide nor his teacher had any knowledge of our history, and I made the instantaneous decision to keep it to myself. I smiled at Anthony, and he kept his silent glare, seemingly searching my face to see any intent on my part to bring it up. In just a moment, I was left alone with Anthony in the hallway.

I immediately got right down to business showing him what I wanted done. "Okay, here's what I want you to do. Just carefully pull these pictures down from the cork strip and remove the staples."

I glanced at him. He was still staring at me, that emotionless, dark, glare that could have sent chills like a shockwave through me. But I turned quickly back to the task at hand.

"And after you remove the staples, just make different piles for the projects, and if there's time, I'll show you how to put them in the folders. And thank you so much for this help."

I glanced at him again as I turned to go back into my classroom. Those cold eyes were still locked on mine, and as I quickly summoned a smile from deep within me to at least offer before I sought refuge behind the door, he spoke. "Wait," he said.

I felt like I had touched an electric fence. His stare was familiar, as was his silence, but I realized I had never heard his voice. I stopped and turned back to face him.

"I'm sorry," he said.

I smiled again at him and just gave his shoulder a pat. There was no need to say anything more.

And at that moment, Anthony taught me the power of forgiveness and grace.

Jamarr

It was a beautiful Saturday in early June. I had taken my seat high in the stands at the local high school, with envelopes in my lap, anticipating the start of the graduation ceremony.

The day before, I had called Jamarr's mother and left word that I would be there. I asked her not to leave before I could see them and give Jamarr his gift.

As the sun beat down, I sat looking over the incoming crowd. One by one, former students spotted me and came running up for a quick hug and a moment of catching up. I always look forward to seeing them all grown up in various stages of their teenage years.

I turned my attention to the field all ceremonially decked out with flowers and rows of chairs. My thoughts turned to Jamarr. I had kept up with him as best as I could through the years but had not had a lot of contact after I began teaching in another county. I had heard that he was now in a wheelchair but didn't know the specifics as to why. I thought of how proud his mother would be when he entered the field to receive his diploma.

My cell phone ringing in my lap broke my daydreaming. I looked at the Caller ID. It was Jamarr's mother, Mornet. I answered excitedly, thinking she was probably calling to tell me where to meet them after the ceremony. I wasn't prepared for the news she had to convey.

Jamarr would not be at the graduation. He had suffered a pulmonary aneurysm and was in Duke Hospital in a deep coma. She said she had tried unsuccessfully to get in touch with me and had evidently been calling the wrong number. She had received my message the day before and was thankful that she had reached me now. She wanted me to know before I heard it in the ceremony, as the principal was going to say something concerning Jamarr during the service.

As the band began playing, Mornet said goodbye and I promised to call her later. I looked down at the envelope in my lap with Jamarr's name written neatly across the front. A tear splashed, causing the ink to run, creating a tiny gray puddle against the stark white canvas.

I heard *some* of the speeches and music that followed. I tried, mentally and emotionally, to be there for the other children I had come to see graduate. Pictures were taken with some after the ceremony, and I passed the envelopes out one by one. I was finally left holding Jamarr's.

Over the next few days, I talked to and texted Mornet frequently. Jamarr was on life support and the prognosis was not good. I sent pictures by email of Jamarr during our happy times in kindergarten.

During our talks, I learned what had been going on in Jamarr's life since I had moved. He had learned how to get around on his prosthetic leg and had even played football. As always, his classmates and team members just adored him. His mother recalled how his football team had set him up in a play so he would be two feet away from the end zone. The quarterback threw him the ball, Jamarr caught it, and stepped over the line to score a touchdown!

Jamarr had also taken up baking. I remembered how he loved our cooking lessons in kindergarten. Once, as we baked biscuits and churned our own butter to go on them, he had remarked that he could eat those every day. His mother told me that he had even baked her a birthday cake.

Jamarr had experienced increasing pressure on his spine. Even with the weight of the leg gone, problems still existed. His prosthesis was found to have been measured incorrectly, and that had resulted in a tragic debilitating scoliosis of his spine. The surgery to correct this problem left him paralyzed. This was the missing link as to why Jamarr was in a wheelchair. Even after this devastating, life-changing event, Jamarr radiated his positive spirit. He wanted to design trucks for the handicapped. Knowing the limitations firsthand, he wanted to help others adjust and obtain independence.

Jamarr was able to attend school in his wheelchair and was on track to graduate with his class. Then the unthinkable happened. He suffered a pulmonary aneurism and slipped into a coma. He quit breathing, and his heart stopped beating on the way to the hospital. He was on life support. That was the point at which Mornet had tried unsuccessfully to reach me.

So now he had missed his graduation and was fighting for his life.

I made the decision to travel to the hospital to see him. My fiancé, Paul, wanted to go with me. As we drove, I talked of Jamarr. He had always been such an inspiration to me and everyone who ever knew him. That smile of his would clear a room of any sadness. I spoke of his mother and grandmother. They had always been there for him, giving care, support, and love. What a blessing they all were to each other. I spoke of the stories Jamarr had shared with me—of seeing Jesus after one of his surgeries. He had become weak and had fallen in the bathroom and Jesus had helped him up. I recall that he smiled when he told me, "Jesus was there. I saw Jesus."

By the time we reached the hospital, Paul felt as if he knew him. As we walked through the lobby toward the elevator, I recalled when, thirteen years earlier, I made this trip to see Jamarr after his amputation surgery. I tried to prepare myself for what I was about to see. For the first time since he entered my classroom on registration day so many years ago, I would not see that beautiful smile.

We entered a sunny room, and my eyes first met those

of Jamarr's grandmother, an ever present caretaker throughout his early years. She was seated beside his bed, as I had seen her doing countless times before. Then my eyes traveled from her to Jamarr. He was turned towards us as we approached the bed, and his eyes were looking straight into mine. There was no change in expression, but I saw him in there . . . behind those eyes.

I smiled and boomed my cheeriest hello. Leaning over, I kissed the top of his head and squeezed his shoulder. I just talked to him. I shared memories of kindergarten, of trotting him to the playground on my back. I shared news of what I was doing now. Then I said, "Jamarr, there's someone I want you to meet. I brought my fiancé, Paul, with me!"

At that second, Jamarr's eyes left mine and moved to Paul at the foot of the bed. After a few moments, his eyes moved back to me.

Yes, I was certain. Jamarr was in there. But he was trapped. Caught inside a body that would not move. I remembered his desire to run as a five-year-old. I felt like crying, but I knew what Jamarr would say if he could talk. "Don't cry, don't cry."

So I stood at his bedside and talked until his eyelids closed in sleep.

I kept in touch with Mornet over the next few weeks. Jamarr had shown a few signs of improvement but had not yet spoken. His family wanted him home, and when a nurse was secured for his acute care, he left the hospital.

He was home, surrounded by his loving family. He never spoke, although in her heart his mother could hear him calling her. He never smiled, but his grandmother could still see it. He never moved, but his brother could still feel the wind as he drove the four-wheeler down the road.

Three months after Jamarr left the hospital, he closed his eyes for the last time. When he opened them again, he looked into the eyes of Jesus.

His funeral was held at the high school. The crowd was so large that the auditorium was filled. As I sat and looked at all the lives Jamarr had touched, I felt so blessed to have known him. He treasured life and taught everyone around him to do the same.

What a tremendous loss we all feel. We loved his smile, his courage, and his sense of humor. He will forever be in the hearts of all who were blessed to know him. I find comfort in the same Bible verse that I taped to his racing stroller thirteen years ago.

> *Isaiah 40:31:*
> *But those who hope in the Lord will renew their strength.*
> *They will mount up on wings like eagles;*
> *They will run and not grow weary.*
> *They will walk and not faint.*

Jamarr has been set free. He is now soaring on heavenly wings.

Adalie

As I write this, it has been two years since "the day the music died." I can still see little Adalie's tear-stained face as my piano was wheeled from the classroom. It has since gathered dust in the corner of the gym.

Life has gone on and new chapters keep unfolding. I asked Adalie to be my flower girl as I married Paul on our mountaintop. I have a beautiful picture of her and me twirling under the stars.

I keep watch as the education system systematically implements one new program after another. As computers replace sand tables and manipulatives, and Book Flix on active boards replace an animated teacher in a rocking chair reading to captivated students, the lights in these children's eyes are dimming. Testing and recorded data are noticed before a teacher knows in her heart the needs and abilities of her students. Children who long to move around are forced to sit in front of a screen and are medicated if they can't do so. Teachers are forced to use computer lesson plans instead of designing a creative learning experience for the students . . . students whom teachers used to have time to get to know personally. Now children have more interaction with their laptops as they greet them each day by first typing in their student number.

Adalie runs to me whenever she sees me at school. I enjoy talking to her and listen to her recalling fond memories of pre-k, of singing, creating her art projects, and rocking in the rocking chair. When she tells me she misses me, I am not sure I am all that she misses. I think she also misses the time when education allowed you to wiggle . . . instead of slowly flat-lining.

ADALIE
THANK YOU
FOR BEING!
MY TEACHER!
I LOVE YOU

April

I walked into the school office and our secretary said, "Betsy, there was a call for you. I took a message and put it in your box."

I thanked her, went over to my box, and pulled out a handful of mail. There was a yellow Post-It note on top with a brief note that read: "Call Irma Garcia," and it gave a local number.

That evening, I settled myself in a comfy chair and made my call. Irma and I talked for a good half hour, catching up on kids, life, you name it. The reason for the contact was to invite me to April's graduation.

I assured her that I would be there. I always tried to attend all of the local high schools' graduations. Somehow, knowing that I started them off makes me want to be there to see how they finished.

It was a gorgeous day. I was there with hugs, wishes, cards, and memories to share. April was beautiful and sporting a gold tassel signifying an honor graduate. How mature she looked. So much poise and confidence.

Her plans for the future included becoming a doctor. I recalled her reluctance to leave that baby doll unattended

in kindergarten and knew she was going to make a fine
doctor. At five years of age, she had been like my right
arm. I could not have functioned without her. She had
been there to help me bridge the language gap between
what I knew and what I couldn't understand. Now her
future would still be building bridges . . . between the
sick and the well . . . between life and death . . . between
despair and hope.

What a beautiful outcome of education.

Armando

After I moved to the adjoining county, I lost track of Armando for a while. When I reconnected with his mother and sisters, I was told he had moved back to Mexico. He soon found me on social media, and he filled me in on the direction his life had taken.

When he arrived in Mexico, he began helping cousins, close relatives, and people in the community with their understanding of English. In 2010, he began a small school in the city. He discovered he had a love for teaching. He said, "I could sit all day long and explain grammar or pronunciation and time would fly by rather quickly. It felt so good."

Armando married, and three years later they had a beautiful son, who reminds me so much of the little boy who entered my classroom so many years ago.

In 2021, he became the academic coordinator at his school, where he hired and trained new teachers. In 2022, he left his position to pursue a second career in medical translation and interpretation.

It's his dream, along with his wife, to have their own English school to continue helping their communities.

I have enjoyed keeping up with Armando and all that he is doing back in Mexico. He blessed me with a heart-warming note on Mother's Day. He wrote:

Happy Mother's Day: To you my most favorite teacher of all time. And don't get me wrong; I had a lot of great teachers in my education. But as time passed, I grew physically, mentally, emotionally, spiritually, and in every other way. I grew. But it was all thanks to my formative years that I began with all the right tools to go on, to persist, to overcome any challenge thrown at me, whether it be from my own decisions or by random, but I went on. I kept beating the drums to the rhythm of my cardiac muscle. Little would I know that my heart and mind would be connected to my most favorite past memories that I had as a child! Like when you invited us to go and play in the pool in the backyard, like when you took care of us while my mother was in labor and the tooth fairy came to visit me while I was there. Like the Christmas tree that I wished for that actually came. Like learning how to tie laces with a shoe box, which is the same way I taught my son to tie his shoes. Like being in your classroom and playing with all the toys.

Happy Mother's Day my wonderful teacher, you're always in my mind whenever I need to remind myself of the beautiful memories I had as a child.

Thank you so, so much.

Epilogue

Today's teachers certainly have a unique challenge ahead of them. They are entering an educational field that is pushing technology on younger and younger students. While the the design of our world may have changed, the way children are designed has not. Their senses still develop in a precise order; beginning with the sense of touch, followed by taste, smell, hearing, and finally sight. If children are forced to bypass this order by having too much visual screen stimulation before the other senses develop properly, problems will arise.

It's my hope that my Little Teachers will inspire educators to provide and nourish all types of hands-on learning for the little ones. Pre-K and Kindergarten children especially need language and manipulative rich environments. Their bodies need to wiggle and move.

These little ones taught me so much. Learning from each other is what teaching is all about. No one can stay in this profession if your heart is not tuned in to the child within yourself and the child you are instructing. I have high hopes and confidence in the eager teachers that I see going into this cherished profession, and I hope that they too will gather years of lessons from their own Little Teachers.